Dealing with Depression

Understanding and overcoming the symptoms of depression

Dr Caroline Shreeve

piatkus

'Dr Shreeve demystifies depression, helps sufferers and their families get free
of the fear and stigma surrounding the illness and gives them lots of self-help
tools for tackling it. She makes it clear that drugs from the doctor and holistic
remedies aren't either/or, and explains how to use them most effectively
together. A very practical and reassuring book'

Deidre Sanders, the *Sun*

PIATKUS

First published in Great Britain in 2005 by Piatkus Books
This paperback edition published in 2010 by Piatkus

A CIP catalogue record for this book
is available from the British Library.

ISBN 978-0-7499-4101-7

Text design by Goldust Design
Edited by Krystyna Mayer

Illustrations on pages 39 and 141 are by Rodney Paull, and on page 36 by Georgie
Birkett. The illustration of Hippocrates on page 34 is reproduced courtesy of Corbis.

Typeset in Sabon by Palimpsest Book Production Ltd, Falkirk, Stirlingshire
Printed and bound in Great Britain by
CPI Mackays, Chatham ME5 8TD

Papers used by Piatkus are natural, renewable and recyclable
products sourced from well-managed forests and certified
in accordance with the rules of the Forest Stewardship Council.

Mixed Sources
Product group from well-managed
forests and other controlled sources
www.fsc.org Cert no. SGS-COC-004081
FSC © 1996 Forest Stewardship Council

Piatkus
An imprint of
Little, Brown Book Group
100 Victoria Embankment
London EC4Y 0DY

An Hachette UK Company
www.hachette.co.uk

www.piatkus.co.uk

Contents

This book is dedicated to my wonderful agent
Mandy Little, of Watson, Little Ltd. Her unflagging
support, patience and sense of humour are among the
finest depression antidotes I know.

About the Author

Dr Caroline Shreeve is a GP with a special interest in mental health. She has trained in psychiatry and worked in general practice in the UK and in Australia. She is the author of sixteen books, including titles on depression, divorce and the menopause. She is a regular contributor to many newspapers, magazines and medical journals.

Introduction

I had several reasons for writing *Dealing with Depression*. Firstly, depression is the fastest growing epidemic in developed countries, and GPs see at least one depressed person every day of our working lives. This may surprise you if you have never been depressed yourself, or known anyone who has been – but the World Health Organization rates it at number five in its list of the top ten disabling illnesses. Figures vary between countries, but studies suggest that up to 25 per cent of all adults are affected at some time. Moreover, the incidence is inexorably growing, particularly within certain groups such as elderly people, students and the unemployed.

Some sufferers deny – indeed, do not realise – what is wrong with them, while others, fearing an emotional disorder 'label', steer clear of doctors until the need for professional help becomes imperative. Treating depression can be frustrating as well as rewarding, and much ground must be covered before its stigma is banished. My account of this everyday, yet serious, condition is directed towards this end. Specifically, I hope that by detailing the brain changes found in depressed people, and their correction by a range of measures, I can persuade doctor-shy sufferers to seek relief, and those who pooh-pooh depression to think again.

Curiously, those who mock sufferers as 'unstable' or 'pathetic', tend also to deny depression's existence. 'It's all in the mind', 'just self-indulgence', 'skiving off work' and 'feeling sorry for oneself' are common slurs, perhaps the more hurtful for their frank inaccuracy. While the term depression may often be misused to represent boredom, bereavement grief or PMT, no one who has seen a severely depressed person – emaciated, dehydrated and doubly incontinent, rambling or mute, nearly dead from exhaustion yet constantly wandering around seeking to kill themselves – could ever forget the image. Nor could they quell their amazement at the 'miraculous' recovery intensive hospital treatment can bring.

The fact that few laypeople get to witness depression's most ghastly visage is no reason to deny its existence. It's easy to feel superior if we ourselves are lucky enough to be able 'always to soldier on, whatever life throws at us'. But depression can descend from the firmament, wiping that smugness from our faces. This illness is a great leveller; none of us is immune to it, and for many it arrives as a shock. Chapter 1 looks in more detail at what depression *is*, and the feelings involved.

Aside from the jibes of its detractors, depression can present major problems in managing and caring for patients. Certainly, some accept what's wrong with them, discuss the treatment options and settle down to take their medication and/or have some psychotherapy. Others, however, reject the diagnosis, deny that they need help and back out of the consulting room, claiming to just be a bit tired and that a holiday will put them right. Others still make an appointment with their doctor armed with a diagnosis – they have read about depression, researched it on the Internet or chatted about it with a friend, colleague or family member. Sometimes they're right, and those who insist they are clinically depressed when they're not are certainly in the minority, but it can be just as difficult to persuade these people that they're suffering from anxiety, perhaps, or the fallout from an unsatisfactory relationship, as it is to convince truly depressed people to accept effective treatment.

Patients' wishes and views must be respected – yet I do believe that doctors should supply all the information necessary to enable the patient to choose wisely, and help to guide that choice whenever necessary. Depression can be a killer, as I point out in Chapter 2, and it is as discouraging to see a badly depressed person refuse antidepressant drugs as it is to encounter someone with diabetes who 'cannot remember' to take his or her tablets/insulin or to implement dietary changes. The need to treat depression when it is present is paramount. To facilitate this I include a list of internationally accepted criteria defining depression, and a chart to help you decide whether you are a sufferer.

A further motive in writing again on this subject (my first book, *Depression,* was published in 1984) stems from my long-established interest in the function and malfunction of the mind, and my experience of treating sufferers both on the psychiatric wards, and during more than thirty years of medical practice in the UK, Australia and South Africa. Part of my interest doubtless stems, too, from my own experience of depression – I was first diagnosed as suffering from the condition at the age of eighteen – and from my conviction that an eclectic approach to treatment generally works best.

I have developed hints and tips of my own to help me crawl out of the black tunnel that is every sufferer's nightmare. I have been able to refine these over the years, and have shared them with appropriate patients, listened to their experiences and learned much from their personal stories and medical histories. Relaxation methods, a sound diet geared towards a depressive's needs, exercise, meditation and a host of holistic remedies all have their roles to play in relieving a clinically low mood. Helping patients to select the measures right for them, and witnessing the gradual re-emergence of a whole human being from the stultifying darkness of despair has been the most rewarding of all my numerous experiences as a doctor.

My acknowledgement of the importance of lifestyle changes and complementary measures in no way detracts from my conviction of the value of orthodox drugs. These drugs are powerful (they need to be) and all of them can cause unpleasant side effects. But the disadvantages – indeed, the dangers – of *not* taking them when needed, far outweigh the inconvenience of side effects. I always feel angry when I read yet another sensationalised account of their nefarious and addictive qualities: and I believe this image can be overcome by more careful and responsible prescribing.

We GPs *must* spell out to the patient how they may possibly feel when they first start taking the drugs, *and* emphasise the importance of returning to the surgery to report on progress. Patients need to know that depression takes us all in different ways, and that metabolic and psychological needs vary, to an extent, between individuals. There are several classes of antidepressant commonly in use, and each class affords a wide selection of possible forms and brands. A change may be needed from one to another before recovery starts. It is absolutely essential for doctors to get patients back to the surgery within the first three weeks of starting an antidepressant course. By this time, any side effects should have diminished (not everyone experiences them in the first place), and their mood should have started to lift.

It is equally important to understand that, regardless what you may read or hear elsewhere, antidepressants do not – they cannot – cause chemical addiction, unlike benzodiazepine tranquillisers and hypnotics (sleepers) such as diazepam (Valium) and temazepam (Temaze), the old-fashioned barbiturates and the powerful, opiate painkillers such as morphine. They *can*, however, cause alarming side effects if a course of them is stopped abruptly, and need to be tailed off gradually over weeks or months – an effect often misconstrued as addiction.

However, the same caution is needed with steroids prescribed for asthma or arthritis, for instance. I have never heard of *them* being criticised and shunned for causing dependence.

The acid test for addiction is the development of tolerance, which means that the body demands higher and higher doses to prevent withdrawal symptoms and achieve the desired effect. Antidepressants simply do not do this. In my opinion, they rank with anaesthetics, antibiotics and anti-viral drugs as one of the great discoveries of modern pharmaceutical medicine.

Chapter 5 takes a look at the different classes of anti-depressants, and at how they act within the brain to alleviate symptoms. First, though, Chapter 3 explains how and where our normal, everyday emotions are created, and how they have developed from primitive reflexes into the sophisticated system we have today. I also look at nature versus nurture in this chapter, at the body–mind complex fundamental to all holistic (complementary) therapies, and at the link between the belief systems of the ancients (from which stem many holistic practices) and our view of depression at the start of the third millennium.

Chapter 4 forms the link between an account of how emotions are formed, and how depressed, negative ones can be produced instead, in response to stress. My argument is that stress of some sort is *always* responsible for depression. I am not referring here to the strung-out feeling we may all experience when we are late for work or the car breaks down, or when we're stuck in a traffic jam or trying to cope with a job, animals, children, a husband, housework, DIY and in-laws simultaneously.

All these familiar stresses certainly *can* tip us over the edge into depressive illness if, for example, our physical health has recently been impaired, or if we have naturally low levels of neurotransmitters (brain chemicals) serotonin, noradrenaline and adrenaline. Some of us, on the other hand, can cope with all these irritants (and more) without any ill effects. The truly decisive factor for most of us is whether we perceive ourselves to be in control of the stressful experiences, or believe that the stress is in control of us.

Aggravants (stressors) we can do something about are relatively harmless. Many forms of stress are highly positive, and can awaken our senses, boost our neurotransmitter levels and make us feel simply wonderful. Stressors beyond our control, however, tend to bring about a state known as learned helplessness, in which we become increasingly less able retain a sense of balance. These negative stressors tend to be highly injurious, and are potent triggers to clinical depression, especially when other lifestyle factors such as poor health, advancing age, being a student and poor nutrition (all stressors in themselves) are also weighed against us.

Nature and nurture also contribute to our vulnerability to depression. Some of us inherit a tendency to the illness, while others are predisposed to depression by traumatic experiences in infancy and childhood.

Having described how we come to suffer from depression and how antidepressants can relieve it by correcting the imbalance of brain chemicals, Chapter 6 talks about psychotherapy and how the different varieties work. I discuss cognitive behavioural therapy (CBT) in the greatest detail, and explain how it provides us with a practical, hands-on method for challenging automatic thoughts (which everyone has), distinguishing between the harmless or useful sort, and others that give us a dim and dismal view of ourselves, our lives and our futures. The reason for this emphasis upon CBT is its accessibility, and the fact that it has been shown in many studies to work best for depression. In fact, CBT combined with antidepressants usually produces the best results of all.

Chapter 7 looks at simple, homespun (but nevertheless highly effective) methods of helping ourselves. There are always going to be *some* depression sufferers who eschew all drug-related and psychotherapeutic help, and this chapter was written with them in mind, as well as those inclined to try a combination of conventional medical treatment, holistic therapies and other self-help techniques. The latter focus upon positively influencing our attitude, banishing negative emotions and challenging self-generalisations, and include techniques such as despatching your depression with the aid of an emotions diagram, and dealing with specific negative emotions, such as shame and guilt.

Chapter 8 looks at physical therapies – how we can help ourselves with diet, exercise and other means to combat depressive illness. Certain foods and food combinations promote the brain's production of mood neurotransmitters, and all the foods mentioned are healthy ones that you probably already include in your eating plan. Many of us lose our appetites when low moods strike, so it is particularly important to select the best foods for body and brain function.

Exercise may be the last thing you feel capable of when depressed, but it is heartening to know that every little bit of exercise taken helps, and that an aerobic workout can raise the blood levels of brain neurotransmitters *and* endorphins, improving mood, well-being and overall body function. Additionally, Chapter 6 details the age-old mood benefits of hydrotherapy, aromatherapy and specific mood-raising essential oils and resins, and massage. Also discussed are herbal remedies (St John's wort and others), the wonderful Bach Flower Remedies, which are growing daily in popularity, and homoeopathic remedies, which can be obtained from a qualified practitioner or over the counter.

The final chapter examines relaxation techniques. These include the standard method of deep muscular relaxation, a method I have devised myself to achieve the same effects slightly more quickly, and a plan for inducing relaxation 'in a moment' when faced with a challenging situation. I also examine yoga and include specific asanas (poses) that can help depression sufferers; and take a look at t'ai chi, which is both wonderfully relaxing and empowering, and at meditation – a simple type and the better known Transcendental variety. Throughout, the main points of the book are illustrated with case histories that shed light on different people's experiences of depression and how they overcame it.

In conclusion, I can assure you that – while an eclectic approach from an orthodox doctor may surprise you – all the therapies and methods described in *Dealing with Depression* have substantially helped many hundreds of my depressed patients. I look forward, with my warmest wishes, to their doing the same for you.

CHAPTER 1

What Is Depression?

We all feel sad at times. Loss, failure, injustice and ill health are all part of human experience. Joy and sorrow, growth and decay, light and darkness counterpoint one another throughout the natural world, and the negative aspect of each pair plays as valid a role within the overall scheme of things as its positive counterpart.

We are all aware of this, at some level. When things are going badly for us, and we feel abandoned and misunderstood by those to whom we normally turn for comfort, we still know that the bad luck is bound to end. 'What goes around, comes around' has many meanings, one being that, however adverse our circumstances, good times will eventually return. With hindsight, we may even recognise that we've grown, are stronger and have gained insight into ourselves and others. Occasionally, negative experiences turn out to be blessings in disguise, at first challenging and then enriching our lives.

Sometimes, however – especially for those of us who are prone to depression – hanging on to hope becomes increasingly difficult. Tussling with an uncongenial job, mounting debts, an unsympathetic boss, interfering neighbours or warring family members can become intolerable. And if this bad patch in our lives is suddenly darkened by the emotional trauma of bereavement, say, or financial loss, we can start to fear for our survival. Platitudinous reminders of a light at the end of the tunnel seem irrelevant and delusional, and we become increasingly convinced that no one understands what we are going through.

As depression develops, the question of 'how to go on' gradually becomes eroded by the realisation that we no longer have the strength to try. Perhaps we no longer even care. The point of life has vanished, we can strive no more, eternal night is falling. The pain is indescribable, yet we haven't a single scratch to show for it. Unchecked, depression can kill – our spirit or soul, our mental faculties and, sometimes, our physical selves.

Many of us weather our personal storms without becoming shipwrecked or, even more remarkably, losing our sense of humour. Growing numbers of us, however, either capsize or are swept off course into the uncharted seas of depressive illness – a phantom-grey world of physical and emotional symptoms where 'self' as we knew it seems doomed to wander for ever.

This may sound melodramatic, but listen to anyone you know who has suffered from depression, and pay no attention to cynics who claim that depression is people 'feeling sorry for themselves'.

Real depression is no more the 'fault' of those affected than is diabetes, bowel cancer or a stroke. It is a recognised medical condition with specific signs and symptoms, and it's the fastest growing epidemic in the developed world. The World Health Organization (WHO) ranks depression at number five in its top ten list of disabling illnesses. According to Department of Health figures, around 20 per cent of women and 14 per cent of men in England suffer from depression at any one time (the figures invariably rise before Christmas each year). The Mental Health Foundation estimates that a figure of one in four UK adults is closer to the mark.

A study called Outcome of Depression International Network (ODIN) published in the *British Journal of Psychiatry* in 2001 compared depression's prevalence in five European countries. The centres in Liverpool (UK), Dublin (Irish Republic), Oslo (Norway), Turku (Finland) and Santander (Spain) included both urban and rural volunteers, adults between the ages of sixteen and sixty-four drawn from election rolls and general practice.

A total of 8,764 people took part in the study, and it was found that the overall prevalence of depression was 8.56 per cent (10.05 per cent for women and 6.61 per cent for men). High-prevalence areas included urban Ireland and urban UK, while a low-prevalence area was identified in urban Spain (research in rural Spain had to be discontinued due to lack of funding), and all the other areas were of medium prevalence.

In the US, a similar number of one in ten people suffers from clinical depression at some time in their lives. Moreover, the illness costs Americans 43.7 billion dollars annually in worker absenteeism, reduced productivity and health care. Australian figures for depression, meanwhile, show an overall prevalence of 16 per cent, affecting one in six men and one in four women.

As well as affecting comparable numbers of people in developed countries, depression is much more common in certain groups of people, such as students, elderly people and the unemployed. We look at some of the reasons for this in Chapter 3.

Why some of us become depressed and others do not, in similar circumstances, will become clear when we look at how depression develops (Chapters 2 and 3). Firstly, we need to understand what depression actually is. This is particularly important because every single one of us has the potential to become depressed, just as we have the potential to suffer from any other common disorder. Because I have suffered from depression myself, I know how ill you may feel, and how hard you may be finding it to struggle to cope with everyday life. I am able to assure you that recovery is possible, because I have experienced this myself.

DEFINING DEPRESSION

The way we use certain words in everyday speech often varies significantly from the way scientists use them. Just as many people complain of flu when suffering from a heavy cold, some say that they are depressed when they really mean despondent, disappointed, lonely or bored. These are feelings that can fluctuate from minute to minute, whereas mood is more stable and more deeply rooted. Your mood colours your views of the past, your attitude to the present and future, and your ability to cope with adversity. Some psychologists have compared mood with a pond, and the emotions with waves rippling across its surface.

An abnormally low mood is the underlying problem in 'real', or clinical, depression (which is what this book is about), and it's light years away from the attack of the 'blues' with which it is occasionally confused. It differs from bereavement grief and from fatigue, lethargy and mental exhaustion (although these can all figure in depression) just as it does from anxiety and from the boredom and stress that caring for small children can bring. It certainly isn't failing to win at Bingo or the Lottery. It's not an unhappy relationship, money worries, hating your boss, being bullied at school or failing to lose weight – although all these can act as triggers. Above all, depression lacks respect for birth, race, gender, creed, rank, intelligence or education.

Spike Milligan suffered from manic depression (where the mood can swing erratically between lows and highs), and Catherine of Aragon was pitifully downcast – almost suicidal, in fact – before marrying Henry VIII. Winston Churchill had to battle with dark despair, which he referred to as his 'black dog', and Sylvia Plath and Virginia Woolf were clearly depressed when they took their own lives.

Depression lasts longer than uncomplicated grief, and has more serious and further reaching consequences. Most importantly, depression influences our lives at every level – not only our mood and emotions, but also our thoughts, concentration and memory, and our bodily functions. The most intense (non-depressive) wretchedness spares our intellectual and physical faculties, or at least impairs them comparatively briefly. Even the terrible affliction of bereavement grief gradually diminishes along a recognised path of milestones as positive thoughts slowly return and recovery gets under way.

What depression ISN'T

Here is what depression is not:

• Feeling down in the dumps
• Losing your temper
• Bereavement grief
• Fatigue
• An unhappy love affair
• Lethargy
• Money worries
• Mental exhaustion
• Problems at work
• Poor concentration/a spell of being uncreative
• Being bullied
• Boredom
• Being fat
• Stress
• Disappointment

What depression IS

Now here's a questionnaire relevant to the most important symptoms occurring in depression, which you can use to help you decide whether you are a sufferer. If you feel you are, you are then in a position to decide whether to seek medical help, or go straight to the self-help tips in the following chapters (most often, people combine the two). It should also help you to see that, in suffering from depression, you are not alone.

- **Depressed mood** Have you felt low and depressed, most of the day, nearly every day?
- **Significant loss of pleasure** Have you experienced a marked loss of interest or pleasure in any activities most of the day, nearly every day?
- **Reduced appetite or weight change** Have you experienced a substantial change in your appetite, nearly every day; or unintentional weight loss or gain of more than 5 per cent of your body weight in a month?
- **Sleep disturbance** Compared with how you normally sleep, are you suffering from insomnia, or feeling unusually drowsy – nodding off whenever you have the chance – nearly every day?
- **Decreased energy** Have you noticed a decrease in your energy level – do you become tired more easily – nearly every day?
- **Feeling restless and agitated** Have you been feeling fidgety or had problems sitting still? Or have you slowed down, as though you were moving in slow motion or stuck in treacle?
- **Loss of concentration** Have you been having problems concentrating? Has it recently been harder to arrive at decisions than it was before?
- **Feelings of worthlessness and/or guilt** Are you feeling guilty or blaming yourself for things nearly every day? How would you describe yourself to someone who had never met you before?

Here's how to interpret the results:

More than five depressive symptoms, including depressed mood or loss of pleasure or interest interfering significantly with social, work-related or other important areas of your life *for more than two weeks* = severe depression.

Two to four depressive symptoms, including depressed mood or loss of pleasure or interest interfering significantly with social, work-related or other important areas of your life *for more than two weeks* = mild to moderate depression.

Three to four symptoms of a loss of pleasure or interest, including a depressed mood, which interfere markedly with how you socialise, work or function in other important spheres of your life *for more than two years* = dysthymia or melancholia (significantly lowered mood/ability to experience interest or pleasure).

Definitions like the above are useful to doctors because they make them generally more aware of the forms depression can take, and therefore able to diagnose and treat it more effectively. The questionnaire is clinically detached, and it may seem both cold and colourless (like aspects of the depression itself) because lists of symptoms don't altogether reflect the starkness, complexity and horror of depressive illness on a personal basis. However, it's important to include it here because, besides giving you some insight into your own problems, it is helpful to know which criteria doctors use in assessing mood disorders.

YOUR FEELINGS IN DEPRESSION

Your feelings become intensely negative when you are depressed, due partly to chemical changes in brain cells that cause a fall in the levels of mood-boosting chemicals, and partly to the turn that thoughts tend to take in depression – harping on and on that you are worthless and useless, perhaps, or reminding you of something in your past that you regret saying or doing. In fact, while your experience of depression may be primarily one of sadness and loss of your usual enjoyment in things and people, other feelings are almost certainly present, too.

Some depressed people feel so guilty that they start to believe that they are responsible for all their own and others' woes, and even see themselves as irredeemably evil, rotten, wicked or, at least, useless. You may not feel like this on the surface; perhaps you are more aware of anger directed at others who have abandoned you or let you down. But deep inside, coupled with the low self-esteem and lack of confidence that underpin all depression, rage in some form is invariably present, directed overtly or covertly at the poor, worthless, inept self. The wretchedness that ensues is often so dark and forbidding that despite your most valiant efforts you may think of ending it all.

Identifying a person's 'real' mood is vital in deciding whether or not they have depressive illness, and often requires much patience, time and skilful probing. The veneer some of us assume when depressed – 'the face to meet the faces that you meet' which T.S. Eliot spoke of in his poem 'The love song of J. Alfred Prufrock' – can obscure how we feel not only from professionals and the rest of the world, but also from those closest to us. We have all read newspaper reports of suicides in which the victim's colleagues and family are, tragically, astonished at the person's actions, because he or she had either given no sign of being troubled by anything, or had appeared to come to terms with recent problems.

A low mood, however, though always present in some form, is not necessarily depression's most challenging feature. Life can prove so stressful that we're more conscious of intense anxiety, of our lives spinning out of control, than of real sadness. One man I knew, a thirty-four-year-old fitness instructor, felt very guilty after being made redundant, failing a job interview, falling out with his partner (over money worries) and waiting weeks for test results following a cancer scare. He believed that none of these things would have happened to him if he had been intelligent, competent and more assertive.

Hatred, envy, a desire for revenge and jealousy are not mentioned in the list on page 14; nearly one hundred symptoms of depression have been identified at some time. They do, in fact, seem strange bed-fellows for the guilt, self-blame and loss of confidence characteristic of the complaint; yet they may also be present deep within our subconscious. Rage at others and at ourselves was first described by Sigmund Freud as a classic cause of depression starting in infancy, and although many psychotherapeutic theories have developed since, none that is tenable seriously disputes the importance of destructive fury in generating depression.

Depression affects all of us differently, and one of its enigmas is its ability to arise for no discernible reason. This sort of depression was once called endogenous – arising from within – but underlying triggers are now believed to exist, if only we look carefully enough for them. The onset of depression can strike us utterly out of the blue, flattening our mood, concentration and physical well-being with the force of a fragmenting meteorite, just when everything seems to be going well for us. We *know* (rationally) that we have much to be thankful for – supportive friends, a successful career or work-free retirement, no pressing financial worries, a comfortable home and loving family and friends.

Yet far from feeling contented, we are dogged by persistent bleakness, emptiness and despair, a sense of not deserving to be happy. Our life seems valueless, dead. Unable to enjoy the good things surrounding us, we feel singular and isolated, at odds with the world, valueless and endlessly at fault. This can make us irritable, even angry, with those closest to us, and with life generally. We may come to feel, afresh, great remorse for mistakes we believed we had dealt with successfully, or torture ourselves over minor peccadilloes. Some religious people may feel that God is punishing them for past trans-gressions, while those who are superstitious can imagine that they are being pursued by a vengeful nemesis.

Wretched in the midst of all that we *know* should make us happy – perceiving what we *know* to be 'white' as 'black' – can carry the more imaginative depression sufferer into the

realm of *Alice Through the Looking Glass*. I am not referring here to the delusions and misperceptions that can beset
manic depression sufferers, but to the surreal awareness of
losing interest in, and enjoyment of, those very friends,
hobbies and activities that have always delighted us.

We may, perhaps, have just passed an exam, become
engaged to someone we love and who loves us, worked extra
hard to save for a deposit on our first home and/or bought
ourselves a stylish new wardrobe. We've longed for and
dreamed about all these things and, suddenly, they are within
our grasp. Yet, far from bringing us the happiness and satisfaction we have anticipated, we're practically untouched by
them; our achievements and plans seem pointless.

No wonder we withdraw into a protective shell from our
significant others, all of whom seem perversely 'normal' and,
of course, incapable of understanding our overpowering sense
of bleakness.

A fear – even a conviction – of something being wrong
without being able to put our finger on it, is a common experience in depression. Few of us are entirely satisfied with
our lot, but this dichotomy between knowledge (of our usual
sources of pleasure) and perception (that these pleasures are
no longer pleasurable), coupled with corrosively self-critical
and persistent thoughts, can turn the desire to escape into a
growing need.

A friend of mine from medical school with no previous
history of emotional problems became severely depressed
when facing intolerable circumstances she felt unable to
control. Her story clearly illustrates the problem of negative
feelings in depression. She did suffer physically, from disturbed
sleep and loss of appetite, but stayed mentally alert and
capable, and was mainly afflicted by a deeply depressed mood.
While the situation may be slightly out of the ordinary because
it affected a doctor, the same sequence of events could easily
have occurred to a man or woman in another walk of life.

CASE HISTORY: JANET

Janet S. was the last person anyone believed could wish to kill herself. An attractive girl who qualified as a doctor at the age of twenty-four, she had written a research paper on burns injuries just before qualifying, and dreamed of specialising in plastic surgery.

Janet married Geoff early into her career. Geoff gained First Class Honours in surgery, won the most coveted house surgeon's post at his teaching hospital, and was encouraged to make surgery his career. He found junior posts where the teaching was sure to be excellent, and was tipped to pass the Primary Fellowship (the first postgraduate surgery exam) within three years of qualifying.

But while Geoff's star was rising, Janet's career started to falter. Instead of applying for a senior house surgeon's post on our teaching hospital's burns unit, she took a job in a suburban hospital and announced that she was going to train as a GP. This was years before vocational training in general practice, when general practice was the poor relation among possible career choices.

At first Janet claimed that a career in plastic surgery had lost its appeal. But gentle probing brought a flood of tears, and the real reason for the change. 'Geoff is very unhappy trying to be a surgeon,' she told me. 'He isn't cut out for it. As you know, he always wanted to become a pathologist, and if he goes on with surgery, he will have a nervous breakdown.' Geoff's severe stress was making him withdrawn, angry, unkind and extremely demanding. He had also taken to wandering the streets at night wearing just a coat over his pyjamas, and blaming Janet furiously for having affairs with fictitious people.

'There is no room in the family for two hospital consultants,' said Janet. 'The stress, the exams, the competition, the killer hours, having to live in hospital quarters! When Geoff's off duty, he wants to come home to me, and a cooked meal, and a clean, tidy house. I have to do this for him . . .'

Janet's other friends and I tried to persuade her to go on with her surgical training, at least until Geoff had changed careers and was emotionally more stable, but she was adamant. Two months later she joined a general practice in West London where, she assured me, she was happy.

Janet seemed to be coping, and even convinced some of us that she was enjoying being a GP. Then, on the day Geoff heard he had passed his first pathology examination, he came home to celebrate and found Janet deeply unconscious. She had taken a combination of anti-vomiting tablets and digoxin (heart tablets), and injected herself with a large dose of insulin. Her expertly planned suicide bid very nearly succeeded.

I felt so guilty about Janet's desperation. Her deep depression had escaped the notice of her family and friends – especially the medically qualified ones. 'It's not your fault – not anyone's,' she told me. 'I've tried so hard to like general practice, but I cannot bear it. I think I am going insane – I cannot leave work behind when at home; in fact I spend all my off-duty hours dreading having to return. I've lost interest in old friends, socialising, reading, swimming. Geoff and I haven't made love for months – I just can't face sex. I just don't want or need anything. I wish he hadn't found me in time . . .'

Janet's depression improved with the antidepressants then prescribed, and a course of psychotherapy. She never did return to general practice but, instead, took a series of locum posts in hospital clinics offering suitable hours and no prospect of career advancement. She still suffers from depression occasionally, but her attacks are far milder than they were since she started a course of SSRI medication (*see page* 67). She also uses a number of the self-help hints I will discuss later in the book.

YOUR THOUGHTS IN DEPRESSION

The poor self-esteem and lack of confidence that predispose you to depression also encourage pessimistic thoughts and beliefs. We will look more closely in Chapter 5 at negative thinking, but I discuss automatic thoughts here to illustrate the central role they play in depression.

When you are faced with circumstances that challenge or threaten you, your central nervous system puts you on high security alert and you tend to jump to conclusions. Automatic thoughts – which everyone has – flash into your mind without a shred of supporting evidence, suggesting various plausible explanations. The thought you choose to 'believe' determines how you feel, and how you cope with what has happened.

Suppose, for example, that you go to the station to meet your partner/lover. You wait near the ticket barrier, the train comes in and this person is not on it. Several possibilities might occur to you, for example:

• You've mistaken the date or time – you're *anxious* until you have checked.
• They've forgotten your date – you're *disappointed* because they don't care.
• They have gone off with someone else – you're *jealous* and *angry.*
• They've simply missed the train – you're *glad* that you can go home and *relax*!

Automatic thoughts can rush onwards so quickly that you experience them more as visual images than as thoughts. If, for example, you believe the secret lover scenario, then you may concoct a graphic fantasy of their going out to dinner, dancing, kissing – to the point where you can actually *see* them making love. In fact, the whole process can occur so rapidly that you are conscious only of the emotions with which you are left. Standing at ticket barriers may make you feel anxious or cross, without realising why. Slowing down and scrutinising automatic thoughts can help you to spot the rogue, or negative, ones.

Often, a sort of dialogue starts up inside your head. In the present example, perhaps you list your grievances against your lover, and go over the accusations you'll hurl at them when you get the chance. When you are depressed or about to become so, internal dialogues or conversations between various trains of thought tend to converge from widely different starting points upon a few, deeply negative conclusions concerning yourself and your world. Automatic thoughts can multiply in people prone to depression, then spiral out of control into depression itself.

Depression also plunders drive and motivation, slows down the rate at which we think, attacks concentration and targets short-term memory. The combined effect on our coping skills can be profound. A depression sufferer will not necessarily experience all these symptoms, or suffer from them in the same degree. But just failing to retain small, everyday incidents, stalling at simple decision making and problem solving, can themselves have great nuisance value.

Rows of figures literally do not add up. Reports, letters and instructions make no sense. We lose the thread of conversations, and written words that usually flow into emails, diaries and shopping lists dry up at source. Caring for children or other dependants can become a nightmare, especially where their safety depends upon our constant vigilance. Being mentally below par often brings criticism and bad feeling from bosses, colleagues and clients, and of course from spouses, partners and older children, who expect us to function normally.

Some depressed people fear that they are developing Alzheimer's disease, and this anxiety – which itself further impairs memory and concentration – aggravates their depression. Ironically, there are mental tests and exercises that can help elderly people, or those in the very the early stages of dementia, to combat a decline in memory and concentration, but they are rarely of use to depression sufferers who, due to their low mood and inertia, lack the energy and will power to pursue them. The next two case histories show the distress that depression-linked thoughts and brain power caused to two quite different sufferers.

CASE HISTORY: LUKE

Luke W., aged twenty, experienced the emotional and physical effects of depression, but it was the intellectual and cognitive symptoms that finally persuaded him to seek medical advice. Luke had been reading physics for a year at university when the sudden death of his sister in a swimming accident, a long bout of glandular fever, financial problems and other stress factors combined to send him spiralling into depression.

At first, Luke attributed his low mood, lethargy and exhaustion to returning too soon after a viral illness to his studies, rugby practice, late-night parties and generous alcohol intake. But he soon realised that his thoughts and intellectual abilities were way below their normal standard. Having always been bright at maths and theoretical physics, a first degree combining these two subjects had been his obvious choice. Now remembering lectures and other information was starting to bother him.

'I'm terribly worried,' Luke told me. 'I'm forgetting formulae within minutes of learning them, can no longer follow simple mathematical proofs and this week could answer only two of the equations set by my tutor. Normally I solve eight or nine in less than half the time. My father died of dementia two years ago – could I possibly have inherited it?'

I was able to reassure Luke that dementia is not inherited. He admitted feeling low, sleeping badly and losing his appetite, and the whole picture he built up for me strongly suggested post-viral depression. I also discovered that Luke's problems with mental function had spilled over from the classroom into other, less challenging areas. He had felt irritated, he told me, about failing to follow the plot of a recent James Bond film and solving a crossword puzzle of the type that had recently been no problem to him. It had also taken him 'ages' to sort out the change for a recent small purchase.

It was no wonder that this very bright boy had panicked at his temporary loss of brain power. A further two months on 'light duties', plus a short course of antidepressants and basic lifestyle changes, soon restored him to normal.

Luke's trigger to depression was his viral illness, on top of the other stress factors such as the loss of his sister. Depression interferes with memory, concentration and puzzle solving and, unaware of this, he became threatened by the unwelcome experience of lagging behind in his studies. His automatic thoughts doubtless suggested various explanations (for instance that he had returned to his ordinary lifestyle too early), but the problem persisted and his thoughts became increasingly negative, culminating in a fear of dementia. Reassurance and advice to slow down his return to full-time occupations settled this fear, and his thoughts returned to normal and his depression lifted.

The next case is that of a forty-eight-year-old woman going through the menopause. She had consulted one of my partners about hot flushes and night sweats some six months earlier. Only now, though, had she plucked up the courage to discuss her 'weird thoughts'.

CASE HISTORY: ELIZABETH

Elizabeth R. told me that she had felt 'depressed' recently. 'I feel hopeless and useless, have no energy and can't make the effort,' was how she put it. 'But what I am really bothered about, Doctor, are the weird thoughts and ideas that just pop into my head.'

Elizabeth had started to fear that she was being punished for 'sins from the past'. These would seem trivial by most people's standards; they included, for example, going through her husband's jackets when she feared he was having an affair, and smacking her young twins when they were naughty.

'I've coped up till now with my job at the school, and thought I was a good wife and mum,' she went on, starting to cry. 'But now I'm scared I may have scarred the children emotionally for life, and wrongly suspected an innocent man. If he ever does leave, it will be my fault for driving him away.'

I also saw from Elizabeth's notes that she'd had several weeks off during the previous twelve months with vague complaints such as 'stress-related illness'. 'I did not have anything physically wrong with me,' she admitted. 'But I developed problems with my short-term memory, and I've lost all confidence at work, although I have managed the school office for ten years.

'I've begun to believe that I'm stupid – that the head teacher would discover that I was a fraud, and that I might be summonsed for deception. I thought when it all started that if I had some time to myself, the problems would just go away.'

They didn't go away. Elizabeth's mood was very low, she was sleeping badly, had gained two stone due to comfort eating and was plagued with these and similar negative thoughts, as well as with poor concentration and lack of mental energy. I referred her for a specialist's opinion to eliminate other, less common mental conditions that can also cause strange thoughts, but he confirmed my diagnosis of depression. Counselling and medication were both required to restore this naturally efficient, competent woman's usual mental powers and self-assurance.

Elizabeth's case clearly shows how severe depression symptoms can respond to antidepressants and to talking things through quietly and rationally with somebody trained to listen. It was about nine months before she was entirely well. The ideal would have been antidepressants plus cognitive behavioural therapy (CBT), which helps to identify and challenge negative thinking, because this combination works better than any other single or combined form of treatment. In this case, however, there was a waiting list of nine months for CBT, so I referred Elizabeth to an experienced counsellor with a particular interest in women's emotional problems.

YOUR BODY IN DEPRESSION

Some people with depression suffer as much, if not more, from the physical symptoms typical of depression as from the psychological ones. Depressed feelings, thoughts and physical symptoms all tend to occur in moderate to severe depression, but what troubles people most depends upon their individual make-up and how it is affecting their lives.

Disturbed sleep

This is one of the most important and most troublesome features of this illness; the form it takes depends upon your type of depression. Anxiety, a common occurrence in depression, can prevent you from falling asleep at night, leaving you tossing and turning into the small hours. Sound sleep often follows, but many sufferers complain of being kept awake by worries and fears, and thoughts that revolve in their heads at ever increasing speeds (negative thoughts fuelled by anxiety often flow quickly – it's our everyday rational thoughts that are slowed down as a rule). Fatigue and drowsiness the next day can be severe, and interfere with daily routine.

People with depression with no apparent cause tend to fall asleep readily, yet wake after two to four hours, often as early as 2 am or 3 am. They then remain awake until dawn. This pattern also causes daytime drowsiness, and can bring great discomfort to anyone longing for the brief oblivion that sound sleep brings. Both types of sleep disturbance respond well to antidepressants.

A further depression-linked sleeping difficulty is persistent drowsiness – a person may sleep solidly all night, yet never feel fully awake during the day and nod off whenever an opportunity arises. Sleepiness can be caused by anti-depressants and, when it is, it normally disappears by the end of the second or third week of treatment. Depression-linked drowsiness *not* linked to medication almost always improves alongside other symptoms as the mood lifts.

Loss of, or increase in, appetite

Loss of appetite may be a feature of depression, alongside a lack of desire for other life-sustaining activities such as social-ising and companionship, relaxation, partaking in your usual pleasures and love-making.

Constipation often results, because eating less produces less waste material, and because depression itself slows down the digestive processes and bowel activity. Advice normally spot-lights the patient's diet and usual eating habits, at the same time focusing upon the wider picture. Any unintentional weight loss in depression is worrying, and it is sound medical practice to monitor a patient's weight when their appetite loss and/or depression is severe.

Small, frequent meals or nutritious snacks (in combination with other treatment measures) can help to recharge a flag-ging appetite; healthy, affordable treats can have a similar effect. (Depression sufferers in general find it very difficult to be kind to themselves, and give themselves treats.)

Conversely, some depression sufferers turn to comfort eating. We all know that significant appetite loss is dangerous and can be life threatening; but comfort eating, in my experience, causes marginally more grief. Stuffing ourselves and snacking on choco-late, biscuits, other junk food and high-fat snacks piles on the pounds. We then feel less attractive – and guiltier – than we did before. This vicious circle – the more we eat, the fatter we get, the more repulsive we believe ourselves to be, so the more we turn to comfort foods – can be extremely hard to break out of.

The long-term consequence of comfort eating is becoming very overweight, with all the attendant risk factors of increased blood pressure and cholesterol, and a greater chance of suffering a stroke and heart attack, arthritis, back problems, diabetes, infertility and certain types of cancer, such as breast, ovarian and womb cancers. If you are affected, you will doubtless have found the immediate effects most unpleasant, too. Nausea, vomiting, diarrhoea, wind, indigestion, stomach ache and painful gall bladder inflammation are all common consequences of being very overweight.

Other common physical symptoms you might experience in depression – some medication-linked – include headaches, dry mouth, a bad taste in your mouth, bad breath, and vague aches and pains in your muscles and joints. Increased alcohol intake can be another pitfall for regular depressed drinkers because the temptation to boost one's mood artificially and temporarily with a quick drink can reach mammoth proportions. The following case history is that of Jodie McS., aged twenty-four, who suffered badly from the physical symptoms of depression.

CASE HISTORY: JODIE

'I feel terrible, Doctor,' said Jodie on her first visit. 'As you know, Ben and I got married a year ago, and we have been thinking about starting a family. We haven't any real money worries – my job as a librarian is going well, and Ben, a pharmaceutical company rep, was promoted shortly after we returned from our honeymoon.

'The problem is that I can't seem to stay awake. The library gets very warm and quiet during the day in term time, and three times in the past fortnight I have fallen asleep at my desk. My boss is very understanding – she puts it down to late nights, clubbing and staying out late at night, but that's fantasy! We haven't done that since we were teenagers. I am just drowsy all the time, partly I suppose because I wake up so early – three in the morning, usually – and although I go to bed at around 10 pm, I am getting on average only five hours' sleep.

'Ben and my parents are also worried about my weight loss. Mother thinks I am still dieting, but I got down to a size twelve before the wedding and do not want to lose any more weight. But I've no appetite . . . I can't eat my lunchtime sandwiches, and in the evenings and at weekends I only pick at my food. I have no energy at all, and as for love-making! Our love life was always excellent but now I just do not want to know. Ben gets either very concerned or very irritable about it.

'I feel like nothing on earth, and wonder whether I might be depressed. We looked it up on the Internet, and I seem to have some of the symptoms.'

Further questions and tests showed that Jodie's thyroid gland, sexual hormones and blood picture were normal (see Chapter 3 for physical causes), and produced no evidence of anything being physically wrong. Most importantly, her weight, which had been around nine and a half stone (60.45 kilos) a year ago, was now eight stone (50.90 kilos) – a loss of twenty-one pounds (9.5 kilos), or just under 16 per cent of her body weight.

Over the course of the next two consultations, however, I did learn from Jodie that while she really did want children, the idea of them brought up distressing childhood memories of physical abuse by an uncle.

As far as Jodie was aware, only her parents knew about this. And while she longed to confide in her husband, she still felt guilty about what had happened and feared how Ben would take it. Jodie had not received counselling after the abuse was brought to light, and I suggested she contact the Sexual Abuse Helpline to arrange to talk to someone. Meanwhile, I made some suggestions about her diet and nutritional supplements, started her on an antidepressant and got her to come and see me at fortnightly intervals to be weighed and to chat.

The counselling helped Jodie to accept that what had happened to her at the age of seven was not in any sense her fault. She then plucked up courage to confide in Ben, who was as supportive and loving as anyone could wish. Jodie's depression took six months to clear up, but her sleep improved during the first two weeks; once this had happened, she felt more wide awake during the day.

Jodie's weight, after 'sticking' at eight stone for six weeks, gradually returned to normal as she regained her appetite.

In the next chapter, we'll be able to relate the symptoms we have looked at so far to physical changes in the brain during depression.

CHAPTER 2

The Inside Story

To understand the symptoms of depression, we must look briefly at how brain cells work normally, and how they change when we're depressed, producing the symptoms. This is depression's 'inside' story – the causes within ourselves – as opposed to the external triggers that are dealt with in Chapter 3.

You may, of course, feel like Mole in *The Wind in the Willows,* when he cut his shin on the Badger's doorstop hidden under the snow. 'What does it matter what done it?' he asks the analytical Ratty. 'It hurts just the same, whatever done it . . .'

What does it matter what happens to our brain cells when we are depressed? All you really care about is getting to the bottom of your own, personal depression and learning how to relieve it. Well, firstly, the triggers and causes become much clearer and more interesting if you know how they influence the brain. Secondly, scientifically derived evidence of chemical changes in the brain may convince you – or someone close to you, perhaps, who is sceptical about depression as a whole – that the illness under discussion is not the product of a hypochondriac's fantasy.

OUR GROWING KNOWLEDGE

Our current knowledge of the mind and emotions, though still by no means complete, must surely exceed the wildest fantasies of pioneer biologists. In 1920, William Penfold, a neurosurgeon, shed light on the origin of emotions when he discovered that intense feelings of anger and sadness could be produced by stimulating different areas of the brain of a conscious patient. Newer imaging systems (than X-rays), such as computed tomography (CT) and magnetic resonance imaging (MRI) scans, reveal considerably more detailed views of the brain's structures than were previously available.

CT scans, for instance, which were introduced in the mid-1970s, combine digital computing with a rotating X-ray device to produce refined, cross-sectional images or 'slices' of the body area in question, which (in the case of the brain) show up the skull, brain matter and blood supply with equal clarity. MRI scans can reveal details of cellular activity that the brain has kept hidden over millions of years. Many subsequent research programmes have looked further into the subject.

The study of the mind and emotions now rests securely upon a scientific footing, but as recently as the nineteenth and early twentieth centuries, scientists dismissed emotions as unfit for research because of their subjective nature. They considered our feelings – in so far as they considered them at all – to arise somewhat vaguely in the body, as opposed to rational thought which, they agreed, stemmed from the mind. There the case rested until the mid-twentieth century, when the true origin of emotions was discovered.

WHERE ARE EMOTIONS CREATED?

The emotions (and memory and learning) are now known to arise not only in the brain itself but within a specific area of it – a ring of nerves called the limbic system. This ring encircles the brain stem, the most primitive area towards the base and back of the skull, responsible for regulating life-sustaining processes. Heart rate, body temperature, breathing, digestion, excretion and elementary reflexes are all under its control, and all are commonly affected by intense emotion.

We have all had butterflies in the stomach when jittery, a leaden sensation in the solar plexus when dejected and a pulse racing with passion! The brain and the rest of the body are inextricably linked by both form and function and, as we shall see, today's widely accepted 'integrated' view of the mind–body complex is that the emotions are the combined product of both.

HOLISM, OR THE MIND–BODY FACTOR

This brings us to the holism, or mind–body–spirit theory, on which is based philosophy and healing systems such as Ayurveda and Traditional Chinese Medicine, and which explains the basis of complementary therapies used today, such as homoeopathy, aromatherapy, reflexology and medical herbalism. Holism recognises that each of us is unique and dependent for health upon the harmonious inter-action of body, mind and spirit. This insistence upon balance as a vital determinant in mental and physical health, which Hippocrates first propounded, has persisted for two and a half thousand years.

Hippocrates, harmony and melancholia

Hippocrates, the ancient Greek father of Western medicine, blamed depression on an excess of black bile, melancholia, by which name depression was then known. This early example of aetiology (science of medical causes) was just one application of the 'humours' theory, which may also have originated with Hippocrates, and which played a pivotal role in the history of depressive illness.

This theory stated that health depended upon a state of dynamic equilibrium between the body's four compositional fluids, or humours – black bile, yellow bile, blood and phlegm. Such factors as good nutrition, freedom from excessive stress and a healthy atmosphere were all thought necessary to maintain the status quo. Ill health set in when the natural proportions of these fluids became altered or upset. *Why,* wondered Hippocrates, did some people have too much black bile? *Where* did it come from?

Hippocrates

The fact that we know how depression was viewed in the earliest records reveals two things: that the condition has always been with us, and that a significant continuity exists between how it was viewed in ancient times and what we know about it today.

As a Greek, Hippocrates' rational faculties would have been schooled from early boyhood in the arts of logic and deductive argument. Painstaking observation and case history-taking persuaded him that, *from birth,* one humour assumes a degree of dominance over the remaining three, moulding temperament and influencing health.

In sanguine people, blood predominated, giving them ruddy complexions and cheerful, optimistic, confident natures. Phlegmatic people, conversely, having an excess of colourless, watery phlegm, were usually paler and somewhat aloof, sluggish and self-possessed. Melancholic people had too much black bile, which, besides being an accident of birth, came – like excess quantities of the other humours – from vapours circulating throughout the body from the residues of unsuitable foods.

Although the theory of humours was abandoned in the nineteenth century, Hippocrates' exposition of temperamental types was akin to those we recognise today, and the connection he established between melancholia, nutrition and stress has been proven many times over by studies into depression's causes.

HOW ARE OUR EMOTIONS CREATED?

Our emotions come from chemical and electrical changes that take place within the brain, nerves and body. The limbic system (*see pages 33, 37*) is not only the seat of the emotions, but also a depot of earlier memories stored within a specialised area called the amygdala (almond-shaped part). Like a customs official, the amygdala vets the ID of every single new encounter and situation we experience, checking whether it has 'visited' before. If the experience is a newcomer, then it records and files away details of the emotional response it evokes. If it 'has been around before', then the amygdala matches it up with the emotional response produced previously, regardless of whether or not it was appropriate.

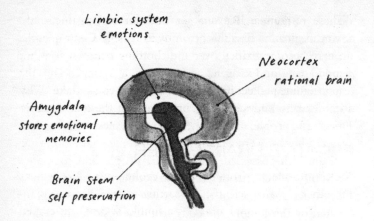

The brain, showing the brain stem, amygdala and neocortex

'Passport' checks of this type were undoubtedly useful to developing primates (ape ancestors) millions of years ago – for instance, seeing a wolf in the undergrowth would initially, and for ever after, trigger flight or fight. But in today's developed societies, most of these primitive responses have become obsolete. Generally we do not murder our nosy, noisy neighbours, however sorely we are tempted to, or run a mile to get away from a bully. We repress our anger and fear, and reap the consequences by harbouring stress and anger that can eventually express themselves as depression.

All this checking and matching occurs repeatedly and within nanoseconds, needing neither effort nor our conscious awareness. But the matching system of present and past experiences is not perfect and, when mismatches occur, they can cause havoc. Childish responses are rarely appropriate in adults, and are often detrimental. Records within the amygdala brain area, where earlier experiences are recorded – of painful childhood vaccinations, for instance – may give rise to a panic reaction whenever a nurse is spotted, or to a phobia of needles and other sharp objects.

These responses, like our sex and survival instincts, are powerful, primitive and impervious to reason. Consequently, we may become baffled by the dichotomy between how we respond to, for example, a nurse, or a syringe, and the response our intellectual faculties would have us make. Why does instinct always get the upper hand in these instances?

PRIMITIVE BRAIN POWER

Pooled information from biologists, evolutionists, biochemists and other research scientists is starting to provide an explanation. The 'emotional brain', or limbic system, developed about a hundred million years ago, a mere watch in the night in evolutionary terms, and a very long time after the primitive brain stem that it surrounds. Equally, the limbic system evolved in primates many millions of years before the development of the outer grey matter, the neocortex, where rational thought arises.

Primates therefore developed emotions a very long time indeed before they developed the ability to reason, giving the emotions far more influence in challenging situations. More importantly, they developed instinctive responses to threatening situations an immensely long time before they developed emotions, making the former of these very much more powerful.

EMOTIONS AND CHEMICAL CHANGE

We have all heard that the human brain is an indescribably powerful and complex computer. It can calculate, store and retrieve far more information, inconceivably more quickly, than any machine. It is also uniquely self-aware, and can both conceptualise abstracts such as love, loyalty and courage, *and* experience the associated emotions. We all take emotions, at least of some sort, for granted, but much painstaking research has been needed to reveal how the brain – a mere five or six pounds of greyish-white jelly – can give rise to, and store, the pettiness and passions that rule human lives.

The main role of the brain here is that of a giant message-relay centre. At a cellular level, everything we do, from going to the lavatory and falling in love, to running a marathon and filling in a lottery ticket, is triggered and co-ordinated by signals, or nerve impulses, passing like emails between the brain and target body areas via long and complicated nervous pathways.

For example, in a relatively straightforward process like breathing, nerve impulses are rapidly and continuously 'emailed' from the respiratory centre in the brain stem, along the selected nerve pathway, down the spinal cord and thence to the autonomic nerves controlling the diaphragm and lungs. This is why we are able to breathe both while asleep and while awake and otherwise occupied. An emotional and physical experience such as falling in love is much more complex, bringing into play such inter-reacting factors as sexual stimuli, past-experience matching, pituitary and sexual hormones, and the brain's mood chemicals.

Pathways from and to the brain, however, are not continuous: that is, a nerve impulse 'email' does not just start with the stimulus at one end and travel without interruption to its target area. Impulses have to navigate an immensely intricate plexus of nervous tissue; and the pathways themselves consist of millions of nerve cells (neurones) lying end to end, communicating with (although not actually touching) one another across minute, fluid-filled, gaps or synapses.

A nerve impulse triggers the release of chemical molecules, called neurotransmitters, from the end of the neurone along which they are travelling, into the synaptic fluid (*see diagram overleaf*). The molecules carry the message impulse across the synapse and then anchor themselves to specific points of attachment, called receptor sites, on the adjacent end of the next neurone in the pathway. A suitable metaphor for this is a relay race, where the second of three runners accepts the

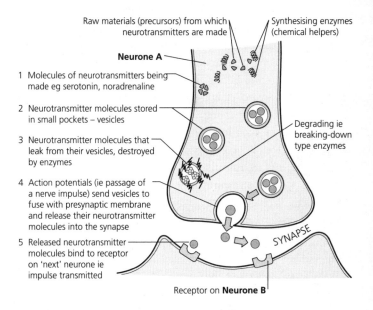

Raw materials (precursors) from which neurotransmitters are made

Synthesising enzymes (chemical helpers)

Neurone A

1 Molecules of neurotransmitters being made eg serotonin, noradrenaline

2 Neurotransmitter molecules stored in small pockets – vesicles

3 Neurotransmitter molecules that leak from their vesicles, destroyed by enzymes

4 Action potentials (ie passage of a nerve impulse) send vesicles to fuse with presynaptic membrane and release their neurotransmitter molecules into the synapse

5 Released neurotransmitter molecules bind to receptor on 'next' neurone ie impulse transmitted

Degrading ie breaking-down type enzymes

SYNAPSE

Receptor on **Neurone B**

Nerve synapse and passage of impulse from Neurone A to Neurone B

baton from runner number one, and carries it with him for a space, to pass on to waiting number three. The molecular binding at the receptor sites, unique for each variety of neurotransmitter, sets off chemical changes specific to the activity or emotion being evoked.

Neurotransmitters involved in mood and emotion, that is the 'mood chemicals', include dopamine, serotonin and noradrenaline. These three substances, known as the monoamines because of their chemical struture, also control sleep, motivation and appetite, and we need adequate amounts of them if we are to remain alert, balanced and capable in the face of adversity.

Monoamine supplies are low in depression, which explains why our mood flattens and sinks, and why we lose interest and a sense of purpose, and suffer from insomnia and appetite disturbances when depressed.

BODY–MIND COMPLEX

Besides the monoamines, hormones produced by glands in the brain (the pituitary) and the body (the adrenals) help to distribute mood-linked data to other body areas. Pituitary hormones and adrenaline and noradrenaline affect the behaviour of big muscle groups, such as those of the upper back and neck, the small blood vessels, and the muscles of the stomach, bladder and bowel. We have all suffered from a tense neck and shoulders after a hard day, had our blood pressure rise or a tension headache develop when stressed, felt sick or wanted to urinate more frequently before a test, or had stomach pains or diarrhoea when badly worried or frightened.

The free flow of hormones, monoamines and other neurotransmitters to open, available receptors seems to be important to remaining happy and calm. Stress hampers this free flow, and the amygdala's activities are thought to include the cellular storage of emotions we have repressed or cannot access. The yearning to talk to someone when worried, and the enormous relief of doing so to people who can listen empathically, can now be explained in terms of cellular action. We actually 'open up' on number of levels when we unburden ourselves to another.

Various psychotherapeutic techniques such as primal therapy (also called rebirthing) – which were popular during the 1970s and 1980s, and which I am not recommending here – are thought to owe any success they achieve to the release of emotions stored before and during birth. Reliving the birthing experience presumably opens up clogged emotional channels, helping to restore calm stability. The abreaction (sparking off of the often violent release of old and repressed emotions) favoured by psychoanalysts of the 1950s and 1960s, and sometimes triggered by an intravenous injection of amphetamine and Valium, worked similarly.

In the final part of the inside story, we see how inherited factors and our past history can affect our serotonin, dopamine and noradrenaline levels.

INHERITANCE

Proud parents of a new baby usually point out features it shares with one or other side of the family. Often the likeness is striking, even within the first few days of life. Yet seeing that a baby has a nose like the mother's, and a mouth, yellow curls and eyelashes like the father's, it's easy to forget that much that an infant inherits is invisible.

We obtain half our genes from each of our parents. These small parcels of DNA provide the blueprints for future growth, and their roles in the development of personality are as important as those they play in a child's future height, body shape and complexion. Nature and nurture – what we bring with us into life, and what we experience once we get here – are both vital to personality development.

Character traits displayed in early childhood may be easy to link with those of either parent. Some may skip one or two generations, so that, say, a grandparent's characteristic may show up in a child but not in the parent related to that grandparent. Regardless of any apparent similarity between a young child's temperament and those of its parents or grandparents, however, evidence confirms that some types of depression – particularly the more severe psychotic or bipolar sort – do run in families.

This is partly due to the many-faceted personality itself; those of us who are anxious, easily stressed, and endlessly eager to please frequently direct anger at ourselves instead of at others, and blame ourselves for our problems (when we are old enough to do so – see Chapter 3), hence becoming liable to depression. But we also inherit a unique neurotransmitter profile, which may include, for example, the poor production of serotonin. (You only find this out a posteriori, when the wages of inherited depression exact their toll.) This may leave us especially vulnerable to the effects of stress, and facing greater problems dealing with depression if it develops.

Some depression that 'runs in families', however, may not

be so much genetically determined as a reflection of the lifestyle that generations of that individual's family have shared, and/or of certain types of parenting. Inadequate or cramped housing, poverty, poor diet, alcoholism, neglect or cruelty, sexual abuse, multiple unsuitable partners of carer parents in single parent families, poor education and employment prospects – just one of these factors, let alone a combination of them, would be likely to promote low moods and depressive illness, both in the parents themselves and in their children.

The following anecdote has remained in my memory for more than twenty years, since working as an agency locum one Saturday morning in a general practice in central London. Two young boys aged eight and ten were brought in by their well-spoken father, who introduced them by name and explained that the younger one was suffering from earache. All three were well dressed, and the two children were exceptionally quiet and well behaved.

I examined the younger boy, who had a middle-ear infection and, just before writing his antibiotic prescription, I said casually to the ten year old – who so far had remained silent: 'And you're all right, are you, Ben? No earaches, no sniffles, nothing Daddy wants me to look at . . . ?'

'Oh *him*!' his father replied scathingly. 'Don't bring Ben into the conversation, puhleese. *He's* the most useless, worthless, hopeless excuse for a son any father could have. There's never anything wrong with *Ben* – and if there were, he would bloody well have to put up with it . . .'

The man spoke with such venom that I was flabbergasted. I watched Ben's pale, set face, which turned a little paler though otherwise remaining expressionless. And I watched the three of them out of the window as they left the surgery and got into a Rolls-Royce parked outside, whose door was opened for them by a chauffeur. I have wondered a thousand times since, how – indeed, if – Ben survived his childhood, and whether he came to suffer from depression.

PERSONAL HISTORY

The 'nurture' aspect of our early development has a profound effect upon the growing brain that, like the rest of us, develops significantly during childhood. Many studies by psychologists and biochemists have indicated that our social interactions in infancy and childhood – how we get on with our parents, carers, teachers, siblings and other family members – influence which emotional response pathways our neurons and neurotransmitters lay down for future use. A supportive, loving and caring experience of childhood acts in developing a brain that differs significantly from that of a child who is made to feel unwanted, useless and even, possibly, hated. Needless to say, it is the latter youngster who will be prone to depression during childhood and later on.

In the next chapter we see how events in our lives that cause stress and negative emotions help to trigger the changes in brain chemicals that bring about depression.

CHAPTER 3

Depression and Stress

We have looked at the chemical changes that occur in the brain during depression, and noted that external stresses – bereavement, relationship failure, financial worries, being too busy at work and/or at home – are the usual triggers. But aren't we all stressed nowadays? What kind of stress most often triggers depression? Can we do anything about it?

SOME STRESS IS GOOD FOR US!

Life today is undoubtedly stressful – not only in 'developed' societies with their manic pace of life, but also in the Third World, where poverty, oppressive regimes, war, crop failure and natural disasters are common. It would be simple for most of us, wherever we live, to reel off twenty, thirty or maybe more aspects of our lifestyles that severely challenge us. But stress also has its positive side.

We vary enormously from each other regarding our goals in life and, of course, in our ability to achieve them. Some of us pant our way up life's foothills, while others scale dazzling heights. But what would life devoid of excitement, danger and focus *really* be worth to us? Not much, surely, to someone like Ellen MacArthur, judging from her successful solo sailing around the world. Nor to Olympic and para-Olympic competitors, more humble sportsmen and women, the child and adult winners of bravery awards, or ordinary people like you and me who have experienced smaller-scale victories – an examination or driving test passed, perhaps, weight lost, cigarettes binned for life, or simply an argument, or a village raffle, won.

Many people love danger and pursue it for its own sake. Extreme sports multiply as devotees devise ever more fool-hardy ways of descending mountains, navigating rapids, falling to earth, living or at any rate swimming with danger-ous animals, and riding the air currents with nothing between themselves and death but a flimsy iron frame and a bit of canvas. Adventure holidays attract all age groups. Few child-ren (or adults) would enjoy fairgrounds if terrifying rides were banned. Horror films and computer games continue to offer armchair excitement, and ghost story tellers and haunted house weekends are booked months ahead.

Positive stress provides thrills through the release within the brain of endorphin, the hormone that gives rise to the 'high' experienced by long-distance runners and others who push themselves to the limit. It also prepares us instantly, through the release of the stress hormones adrenaline and noradrena-line, to fight or flee from danger – a very positive effect if you are fleeing a would-be mugger! The stress hormone surge is also partly responsible for the almost superhuman strength, courage and staying power some people acquire during an emergency; and it 'keeps us on our toes' when we have to act, speak in public, go before an examining board, appear in court or otherwise take part in activities that scare us to death.

You will have experienced the positive and negative influ-ence of the stress response if you have ever had to swerve or brake violently while driving. Adrenaline and noradrenaline, squirted into the bloodstream by the adrenal glands (in the abdomen) immediately you perceive danger, provide your lightning response that hopefully saved lives. These hormones are also responsible for the violent trembling, thumping heart, dry mouth and painful arm and leg muscles that can affect you for a minute or so after the event.

NEGATIVE STRESS

Some kinds of stress, such as bereavement, divorce, major rows and moving house, are recognised by all of us as traumatic and so potentially harmful. But other types, which some of us barely notice, prove highly taxing to others. You may be *driven mad* by a neighbour's dog barking, which would not bother me at all. I *cannot bear* having to listen to pop music, which you may enjoy playing more or less continually. Non-smokers are frequently *enraged* by others enjoying a cigarette. And huge numbers of us become *stressed – almost paranoid* – by tail-gating drivers.

The common element in both types of stress – the general sort, like that coming about as a result of braking in an emergency, and the individual kind that results from our personal preferences – is a lack of control on behalf of the sufferer, and it is this element that makes stress potentially harmful. One of the most irascible of my friends, who is susceptible to all of the above irritants and dozens of others besides, can read quite contentedly within earshot of a noisily dripping tap. When I asked him why, he explained that he could blot it out. Of course, we cannot control tail-gating drivers, neighbours' dogs barking or wayward smokers, but when a stress trigger is within our control, we can afford to ignore it until we choose to deal with it.

'LEARNED HELPLESSNESS'

Research has shown that animals subjected to unavoidable stress behave like depressed people: they become listless and inert, lose interest in their surroundings and their learning ability is affected. Subjection to stresses that the animals *can* control, however, does not have this effect. We behave similarly when faced by uncontrollable stress. People forced to deal with negative stress 'learn', that is react, by becoming 'helpless and hopeless'.

Whether we perceive a stressful situation as manageable or beyond our control is crucial to how we deal with it. Perceiving it as hopeless, or ourselves as too weak to cope, lowers our mood and leads towards depression. We look at this in more detail in the chapter on cognitive therapy (*see page 84*).

STRESS AND GENERAL HEALTH

It is also worth taking on board that misery is bad for our general health, and especially for the immune defence system. A recent study in the United States measured electrical activity in the prefrontal brain area of fifty-two volunteers aged between fifty-seven and sixty years. Each person was asked to concentrate upon a sad or happy event from their past, and a note was made of whether the resulting emotions aroused more activity in the right or left side of the brain area. Individuals with greater activity in the right prefrontal lobe tended to be pessimists who ruminated over sad happenings. Greater left-sided activity denoted more cheerful optimists who took stress in their stride.

The strength of the participants' immune systems was then examined by giving each of them a flu virus vaccination and measuring their antibody response three times over the following six months (a good antibody response means healthy immunity). The immune systems of those with greater left-sided brain activity (the more cheerful ones) were significantly stronger than the immune systems of those with greater right-sided activity (the pessimists).

According to the research team's leader, Dr Richard Davidson, a neuroscientist at the University of Wisconsin, 'This study establishes that people with a pattern of brain activity that has been associated with a positive style are also the ones who show the best response to flu vaccine. It begins to suggest a mechanism for why subjects with a more positive emotional disposition may be healthier.'

Furthermore, active immune defences are essential in warding off malignant diseases. If you are habitually over-whelmed by stress factors beyond your control, and hate and fear change, you may be more susceptible to cancer than optimistic, confident people open to innovations and risks. In a recent study of rats whose results can be extrapolated to humans, the animals with neophobic tendencies (those frightened of new things) were 60 per cent more at risk of dying than the neophilic ones (those who liked new experiences). The daunted ones developed higher stress hormone levels when faced with unfamiliar objects very similar to those seen in children from the age of fourteen months who are shy, inhibited and scared.

In a paper presented to the journal *Proceedings of the National Academy of Sciences* in 2004, the two researchers Sonia Cavigelli and Martha McClintock, from the University of Chicago, reported that the average lifespan of the frightened rats was 599 days, as opposed to 701 days for the bolder animals. Both kinds died from similar causes, that is tumours linked to old age, especially those of the pituitary gland in the brain, which plays a vital role in the control of stress hormone release. However, the confident rats were less vulnerable to age-linked diseases, and better able to survive once they developed such tumours. It was suggested that the high hormone levels in the neophobic rats weakened the immune system or caused free-radical-type damage, and that adverse effects on nervous tissue and the brain may have triggered pituitary cancer or reduced their ability to exist alongside tumours.

We can never be sure that stress is linked with cancer in any particular instance. Nevertheless, here is the story of Anna B., a fifty-two-year-old chartered accountant from New York City, who had never suffered from depression or any other serious illness before being bombarded by more traumatic events within a twelve-month period than most of us face in as many years. The story is told in her words.

CASE HISTORY: ANNA

By the time I reached the age of fifty, in August 2001, I was starting to believe that one really can 'have it all'. Not that I had ever expected as much. But life really was working out exactly as I had always dreamed, and I felt both lucky and grateful to God – or providence – or whomever was smiling so beneficently on me and my family.

Then came September 11. Our son Marcus, a talented musician, had flown to England to take part in an international piano competition which his teachers and friends – and, of course, his father and I – felt he had a good chance of winning. In fact he came second, with a highly commended appraisal by the examiners and the offer of a scholarship to continue his studies in Paris, at the Sorbonne.

Marcus telephoned us immediately with the results. Pete and I, and our two daughters, were so thrilled, and so very proud of him. That was on September 9. He flew back to the US the next day, and on the 11th, went into New York City to see his bank manager about the scholarship funds. His appointment was for 8.45 am near the World Trade Center, and that was the last we ever heard of him. None of his remains has ever been identified.

Pete and I and our daughters simply could not take the facts in – one minute our adored son and brother was a prize-winning pianist with the whole world before him, and the next it was as though he had never existed. I have to ask you to imagine our grief – I cannot find the words. Then, in December 2001, my mother was diagnosed with heart failure. She went downhill very rapidly – I still maintain that this was partly sparked by the shock of losing her grandson – and died, aged seventy-two, on 1st April, 2002.

I guess I was preoccupied with family affairs – and I forgot to keep my ear to the ground on the work front. I had taken three months off after we lost Marcus, and redundancies had been planned, but I in no way anticipated that they would involve me. My feelings when I was told that I would have to leave in September 2002 – with some pension concessions – are almost as hard to describe. I felt the company could have been kinder, considering our loss, but I know this is unrealistic – company executives simply do not think this way.

A month after my enforced redundancy, Pete had a small stroke and had to give up his overtime teaching and take a lower salary. My youngest daughter, Mary-Rose, aged twelve, then found she was pregnant by a boy we had no idea she had been seeing. Finally, Betty, our cocker spaniel, was run over outside our house, right in front of me. Perhaps this trauma haunts me the most – because it is the most vivid.

Anyway, I had been going downhill before my mother's death, and felt that events were simply piling on top of us all – quite beyond our control. And I am afraid that I just gave up – I didn't care any more and did not want to know, or to do, anything. It all seemed so hopeless, and I felt terrifyingly at the mercy of fate. A black mole developing on my thigh turned out to be malignant, and perhaps this was connected to the stress, but I am only guessing here.

Fortunately, a dermatologist caught the cancer in time, and the operation proved successful. But I had to spend two months in a private hospital because I was so depressed, and only now, after months on medication plus cognitive therapy, am I starting to feel back in control.

THE ROLE OF CORTISOL

What gives uncontrolled stress such devastating power? (For uncontrolled, we must also read excessive, prolonged or negative in other ways that we cannot regulate.) Well, when adverse circumstances go on and on, without our finding a solution or adequate coping strategy, as in Anna's case described above, levels of the hormone cortisol rise in the blood. Cortisol, a hormone secreted by the adrenal glands, is present in all of us at all times, and plays vital roles in our metabolism.

Cortisol's useful functions include helping to prepare our fight or flight response. It also combats inflammation, and helps to stimulate the release of endorphins (which as well as providing a feel-good factor, temporarily decrease our sensitivity to pain). Other benefits include its action on fat to provide energy, its assistance with various liver functions, and its maintenance of blood sugar and energy levels within normal limits. However, high levels in the blood sustained over a prolonged period have adverse effects.

Under conditions of harmony and balance, the body regulates its cortisol release according to preset highs and lows closely affiliated to the setting of our body clock. Prolonged high cortisol levels triggered by stress include a weakened immune system, and reduced brain function leading to poor concentration and memory. The activities of our good mood chemicals, serotonin, noradrenline and dopamine, also suffer.

Poor serotonin function

This upsets our body clock, which in turn interferes with sleep cycles, the release of stress hormones and the control of body temperature. Instead of falling asleep with ease and drifting naturally into increasingly deep sleep, we experience less of the restorative type of sleep that we need for physical and mental health, and more of the dreaming variety, which leaves us less refreshed on waking. The familiar morning grumpiness we have all experienced could be less a question of our getting out of bed on the wrong side, than of the 'wrong type of sleep'.

Stress hormone levels are normally higher during the day and lower at night in preparation for rest. Upsetting this rhythm leaves us at the mercy of excessive fight and flight stimulation, so that – unless we're more than usually active physically to work off the effects, exercising or partaking in other activities that demand a lot of energy and thus provid-ing a natural outlet for these hormones – we can feel constantly on edge and anxious, and also have difficulties in sleeping. Raised adrenaline levels have other adverse long-term effects such as high blood pressure, higher risks of heart attack and stroke, stomach and bowel disorders, and in some people a proneness to anxiety-related disorders, such as panic attacks and phobias.

Reduced body temperature control can be a nuisance, espe-cially if you are a poor sleeper. Our temperature normally drops as we approach bedtime, which in turn prepares us to become drowsy and relaxed, and it rises in the morning as we become active. Insomnia can be aggravated by feeling too hot at night, and physical discomfort due to stress or depress-ion can be aggravated by feeling chillier than usual during the day. The following chapters provide suggestions for maximising serotonin activity.

Poor noradrenaline function

Noradrenaline normally keeps us alert, involved and energ-etic. Reduced levels leave us tired mentally and physically, with little interest or enthusiasm in our usual activities.

Poor dopamine function

When dopamine activity is reduced, the production and release of endorphin is also depleted. The pain threshold is lowered, which makes us more than usually sensitive to muscular twinges, minor headaches and other trivial ailments. More importantly, our experience of pleasure declines, as does our interest in people, hobbies and activities that normally fill us with enthusiasm.

The point to remember is that, whether we become depressed due to the cumulative effects of stress, or to habitual thought patterns that sap our self-esteem, or for no discernible reason, chemical changes occur within the brain, generating depressive symptoms. This is why a positive outcome to antidepressants can be confidently predicted in nearly all sufferers. Clearly, identifying and dealing with some of the triggers – such as unresolved bereavement grief, lack of an outlet for pent-up emotions, lack of assertiveness in traumatic relationships – greatly increases the chances of long-term freedom from depression.

WHO IS PRONE TO STRESS-RELATED DEPRESSION?

Just to recap what we've discovered about stress and depression: research confirms that 'intolerable' stress interferes with learning and concentration, and can result in 'learned helplessness'. It has been established scientifically that over a period of time, badly stressed people develop abnormally high levels of the hormone cortisol. This weakens the activity of the three main mood-boosting brain chemicals – serotonin, noradrenaline and dopamine. Can you see now how misguided are the sceptics who hold that depression is 'just a matter of feeling sorry for yourself'?

People within certain social groups experience stresses that make them particularly depression prone.

Students
According to a survey carried out for the Mental Health Foundation (MHF) and published in the *Guardian* on 8 January 2001, 46 per cent of male students and 64 per cent

of female students in Britain experienced symptoms of depression. Figures for a similar student population in 1987 showed between 1 and 25 per cent experiencing significant emotional difficulties. Pauline Fox of Thames Valley University, who conducted the survey, pointed out that it was arguable whether these figures reflected the general population, or whether higher numbers of students really are becoming depressed. 'The student population is far greater and made up of a far wider spectrum of people than ever before, and the pressures are higher with people having to work very hard outside university to earn money. Students' health may also be poorer than others.'

However, an unpublished report by the Association of University and College Counselling, seen by the *Observer* and reported in the same *Guardian* article, clearly emphasised the crisis of mental illness among UK students. Twelve per cent of students at established universities seek counselling at some point during their studies, a rise of 25 per cent since 1996. This far exceeds the students' health service counselling facilities, since only around 4.7 per cent of those in higher education actually receive counselling. Meanwhile, the services 'are being cut due to funding problems just as the demand is rising'.

Besides indifferent health, financial worries and often having to work part-time, reasons for the high depression rate among students include poor nutrition, lack of exercise, drugs and alcohol abuse, and poor socialising skills. 'A' grades in school subjects prior to university entry do not necessarily ease the daunting 'rite of passage' involved in joining an adult learning group, and getting to know and becoming accepted by one's new peers. Familiar faces from school have been replaced by those of strangers; and there is the additional trauma, for many, of leaving home for the first time, and having to deal with everyday necessities such as food shopping and cooking, managing finances and keeping abreast of their course studies.

According to the MHF's research, employers tend to stigmatise depression, which worsens the poor job prospects many students face on graduation. Employers, it seems, 'would rather give a job to an ex-convict than to anyone who admits to having suffered from depression'. This is particularly worrying because the epidemic of depression is set to overtake heart disease, AIDS, malaria and malnutrition within the next twenty years to become the second most common killer in the world after cancer. 'These are alarming statistics,' said Professor Jeffrey Gray of the Institute of Psychiatry:

What one must remember is that depression not only kills through suicide but also leads to an early death in other ways. It changes the structure of the brain and there is evidence now that links it to cancer, infectious diseases, premature ageing and undoubtedly dementia. We are designed to cope with acute stress, the kind that would see someone running away from a lion. But modern stress is prolonged and evolution has not designed us to cope with that. (*Guardian*, 8 January 2001)

Homesickness suffered by students can spiral into depression when they are afraid to seek help for their problem, or turn to drugs or alcohol for solace. This is the story of Roberta, a student who almost did not make it to the end of her first term.

CASE HISTORY: ROBERTA

Roberta was eighteen in the October of her first university term. She told me: 'I was so looking forward to "being an adult". Of course, I suppose I had thought of myself as grown up for the past three years, but I had never worked in a real job, apart from a fortnight at the local sorting office at Christmas, left home properly, or had to look after myself big time as I did at uni.

'Two of my best friends came to the same college, but they were on different courses and I hardly saw them. I was in a hall of residence where most of the others were second- or third-year students, and I felt a bit shy. We also had to share the loos, bathrooms and kitchen, which I wasn't keen on, and when I found there was no room for my things in the fridge, I just avoided buying food that needed refrigeration. I bought lots of fresh fruits and salads, but I was also eating fatty takeaways and crisps and chocolate.

'I was more than 200 miles from home, and missing everyone terribly. I tended not to go to parties – it was too much hassle when I did not know anyone. At first I just studied in the evenings, but it was hard to work in hall because it was always so noisy. Then someone in my year offered me a joint. It made me feel very sick, but I liked the spaced-out feeling and bought some more. I made friends this way, but they were all heavy drinkers – at least I thought so. We'd have a few beers at lunchtime, and more after lectures were finished, and wine with our evening meals.

'I stopped writing home, and rarely rang my family. My course work was suffering – I couldn't be bothered to study, and I came bottom in two tests. My new friends' habits worried me – but I tagged along and was too ashamed to ask for help. I cried a lot, nearly stopped eating, couldn't sleep and started to feel it was pointless. In the end my course tutor spoke to me and got me to contact the student health centre. The doctor there prescribed an antidepressant, and talked to me about the benefits of exercise when your mood's low. It all made sense – as did his suggestion that I needed some time out. There was only a week left of the term, so I went home and told my parents how things were going.

'They were very understanding – only a bit upset that I hadn't confided in them earlier. I did extra work assignments during the Christmas vacation to catch up with what I had missed, and cut way back on the booze. And when I returned to uni, I joined two clubs – the student ramblers' branch, and a fun one several of us ramblers set up, to teach ourselves to cook. Shared meals and outings followed, I made more friends in my second year and life became manageable again – and much more fun. I haven't been depressed since.'

Elderly people

Around one in five elderly people suffers from depression. It is slightly more common among those in residential care, and affects twice as many people as dementia. Many go undiagnosed and untreated, however, and this is particularly worrying because elderly people run the highest suicide risk, and their general health tends to be badly undermined by depression. In ten years' time, nearly 25 per cent of the population will be over sixty, so the problem is almost bound to grow.

One of the chief reasons for this lack of detection of depression is ageism: many of us, including doctors, somehow expect older people to be miserable, and the sufferers themselves are often unwilling to talk about their feelings. Some dislike making a fuss and 'bothering their doctor'; others fear that adding emotional problems to their current disorders will lead to them losing their independence; and many were brought up at a time when depression was rarely discussed, and stigmatised even more than it is today.

Causes for depression in older people range from loneliness, lack of stimulation, losing a partner and falling out with family members, to health worries, poor nutrition, the side effects of medication and deteriorating sight, hearing and mobility, which makes them feel useless and limits their sources of interest and pleasure.

CASE HISTORY: TERRY

Terry was eighty-eight when I went to visit him at the request of Sue, his niece. He still lived alone and 'did for himself', and had declined help from social services after his wife died two years earlier. He wasn't happy to let me in – grumbled that his niece shouldn't have gone behind his back. But when I explained that Sue had been worried about him, he burst into tears.

'The trouble is, Doctor,' he said, 'she came earlier than usual on Wednesday, and caught me crying. The place was a mess – lots of unwashed stuff in the sink, no food in and the cat had messed in the sitting room. I generally have a good tidy up before she arrives, so that she has no cause for concern.

'It's just getting harder all the time to do without Alice. I know she spoiled me, but she'd never let me lift a finger in the kitchen or anywhere else. Now I have to vacuum and dust, remember to let the cat out five or six times a day, pop to the corner shop for food, and then cook it and clear up. I can't seem to work up any interest in all these little jobs. I've lost weight because my appetite is bad, and when I wake up in the morning – often as early as 3.30 am – my first thought is, "Oh no, not another day to struggle through . . ."

'I know I should be grateful for my health – there's plenty worse off than me. But I've been wondering whether to end it all, so that I can be with Alice again.'

Terry had been scared to accept Meals on Wheels or home help because he thought that 'they' might take away his cat if she messed, or have him 'put away'. I was able to reassure him on these points, and persuade him to accept regular help with cleaning, shopping and laundry. The home help was a local woman who put him in touch with another elderly widower in the same block of flats, who was similarly lonely, and they struck up a regular friendship.

These little changes, added to a course of antidepressants over the following four months, gradually brought Terry's low mood and other symptoms under control. He even weathered the death from old age of his cat, and was optimistic enough about the future to offer a home to a stray kitten from the local animal rescue centre, which Sue told him needed a home.

Unemployed people

We all know that unemployment is an extremely stressful experience, and research into its effects in Britain over the last sixty years has shown consistently that up to 40 per cent of unemployed people experience psychological distress. Of course, many people suffer from emotional problems that make it difficult or impossible for them to find or hold down jobs in the first place; but numerous studies agree that unemployment is also a cause of depression and other emotional problems.

The jobless people who have been studied suffered more than their employed peers from low mood, anxiety, dissatisfaction with their present life, general stress, poor self-esteem and hopelessness regarding the future, and their physical health was poorer. There is also a knock-on effect upon the physical and emotional well-being of the partner and children of an unemployed person's family. The salaried spouse (usually a woman) with an unemployed partner has to deal with financial worries, the 'intrusive presence of an unemployed partner at home all day' and trying to keep the family together and thinking positively.

Children's schoolwork tends to suffer and continues to decline as long as the unemployment of the parent persists. This is particularly true of the children of out-of-work fathers, who may become prone to depression, loneliness and increased emotional sensitivity. They also become distrustful of others, tend to withdraw from contact with their peer groups and friends, develop low self-esteem and show antisocial behaviour.

It seems that the mental health damage many jobless people sustain results from their being deprived of benefits working people enjoy, which generally serve as psychological support. These 'unintended' or 'latent' bonuses include having a time structure imposed upon the working day, contacts and shared experiences with others outside the nuclear family, the feeling of teamwork that results from mutual purposes and goals within a group, a sense of status and social identity, and oblig-atory activity.

Employment affording little or no job satisfaction tends to produce similar emotional problems to unemployment. In addition, the negative effects of unemployment can persist after the person is back in work. Re-employed professionals are often underemployed, that is working in posts with poorer salary, more menial work and misuse of their skills. They often worry more, too, about future redundancy because of last-in-first-out practices. One study that followed up a group of previously unemployed people found that those who felt dissat-isfied with their jobs became more stressed and developed lower self-esteem than they experienced while out of work.

The 'legacy' effects of unemployment can make them-selves felt whatever the quality of the new job. The chief of these are the person feeling that their work record is permanently stigmatised, having doubts about their personal ability and self-worth, and experiencing feelings ofpersonal failure.

So many lives could be saved, and so many more people helped to overcome their depression, if they did not fear the stigma of emotional disorders and could easily access professionals with the skills and time to listen to them. Bill, fifty-two, was out of work for over a year after financial problems hit the family-run factory where he had worked all his life. None of his family realised that he was at the end of his tether. I saw him after he had been discharged from intensive care, having tried to hang himself.

CASE HISTORY: BILL

'I expect you'll say I was being silly, Doctor – or else wicked. I didn't want to hurt Charmaine or the kids, but I just couldn't stick another day of feeling so ashamed and useless. Over the past year,

I've applied for something like eighty jobs – first factory ones easy to travel to, and then others, anything – silly distances from home. In the end I was ringing up about street sweeping, litter collection, washing up in cafés and bars. But the answers were always the same: "We're looking for someone younger," and "You're over-qualified, and have no experience." I mean, do you really need youth and experience to wash up, or dispose of rubbish in the local park?

'My wife was great – but her mother started to nag her about providing for the family – we never did see eye to eye. Then our eldest, Wayne, started to truant from school and was found drinking and smoking in the shopping centre. None of the kids had ever been in trouble before. I read him the riot act and he accused me of "bunking off work". I was already feeling depressed and down and this did not help.

'Two months ago I got an interview at a factory twenty miles away. I turned up early and noticed they interviewed all the other, younger, applicants who'd arrived after me first. Finally, when they'd kept me waiting two hours, they offered me my bus fare and said they'd appointed one of the youngsters. They didn't even apologise.

'My mood was going down to my boots and further. I couldn't hold my head up – not in the pub or the supermarket or even in the street. A mate (who's no longer a mate) then told me Charmaine had been seen out with another bloke. Turns out, which I did not know before, that Charmaine had beaten his missus to a job in the local supermarket – the pair of them were mad as dogs about it.

'But I believed him. It hit me so hard, and I couldn't turn to Char for reassurance because I felt that if it was true, she'd lie anyway. So I waited till she'd gone over to her mother's and took twenty paracetamol with half a bottle of whisky and tried to hang myself. Char came back early and found me – I feel so dreadful to have put her through it all. But I've come clean about my depression now, and hopefully I will soon be on the mend . . .'

Many depression sufferers require antidepressant medication and, in the next chapter, we will find out why.

CHAPTER 4

Who Needs Antidepressants?

You, I or anyone else might need medical treatment for depression – we are all capable of suffering from it. All the same, the prospect of taking antidepressants may fill you with horror. Perhaps you have been battling grimly with your low mood, and feel that to accept medical treatment would be a sign of weakness. Perhaps you can't come to terms with the diagnosis of depression because you know people who might ridicule or blame you if they knew – despite you having to agree with your doctor that you are suffering from the symptoms. And please – *do* go to your doctor. We're more knowledgeable about such things than we were even ten years ago, and statistically you are extremely unlikely to come up against a GP who 'does not believe in it'. Rather than 'telling you to pull yourself together', he or she will probably offer you a course of antidepressants if you need it.

Antidepressants are usually essential in the treatment of severe depression, and can also be very helpful to people affected by mild or moderate forms of the condition. They work by raising brain levels of serotonin and other mood-boosting substances; research has shown many times over that badly depressed patients do best on a combination of antidepressants and cognitive psychotherapy and, for many sufferers, anti-depressants are life savers.

THE FEAR OF ANTIDEPRESSANTS

Despite the obvious benefits of antidepressants, those who would most benefit from them are often fearful of taking them. Understanding yet helping people to overcome this fear becomes a bit of a mission for health professionals keen to aid recovery from depression. You see, psychotherapy alone cannot help when you are too sick to benefit from it, and most complementary or self-help methods need some motivation and effort – yet these are often conspicuously lacking when depression holds sway. The concerns about antidepressants that bother sufferers the most are described below. The subjective experience of taking antidepressants and the side effects are covered later on (*see page 65*).

'I don't want to get addicted'

Rest assured that you cannot become addicted – antidepressants are non-addictive substances. They are non-tolerance-forming. This means that your body does not become sensitised to them, or learn to tolerate them and then demand ever larger doses to obtain the required effects.

In this and in other ways, antidepressants differ from drugs such as diazepam (eg Valium), lorazepam (eg Ativan) and temazepam (eg Temaze), which are habit forming and give rise to unpleasant and sometimes severe withdrawal symptoms if a dose is missed or the supply runs out. These tranquillisers and sleep inducers, known as the benzodi-azepines, do play valuable roles in the treatment of clinical anxiety, insomnia and other disorders, but they should be prescribed and taken with great caution. They do not relieve and may even aggravate depression, and are rarely prescribed during this illness.

A word of caution about coming off antidepressants: while you cannot become chemically dependent upon them – and they do not cause tolerance – our brain cells nevertheless become *used to* having them around. Correcting low levels of mood-boosting brain chemicals is a delicate operation, and a course of antidepressants needs to be tailed off gradually over several weeks depending upon the size of the dose and the length of time they have been used. Cases of failure to do this have brought several major antidepressants into disrepute.

Seroxat (paroxetine) made headlines in 2003 when a number of patients complained of traumatic experiences on ceasing to take them. Uncontrollable crying, severe panic, thoughts of and even attempts at self-harm, headaches, nausea, vomiting and profoundly low mood were among the problems reported. These symptoms can be avoided by reducing doses according to a plan agreed between patient and doctor. (*See also* Prozac, *page 66*.)

'I can fight this by myself'

This may be so. But why go to endless lengths and put up with unnecessary misery to achieve something that can be more easily and quickly gained with help? You would not refuse crutches and a plaster cast if you broke a leg, or turn down physiotherapy to help you walk again. We all need to be aware of the advantages and drawbacks of antidepressants, and doctors need to spell these out when prescribing them. If you are depressed and your GP suggests a course, make sure he or she sees you after the first couple of weeks, and every four to six weeks thereafter, to check on your progress. And if you are afraid of the stigma, discuss this, too, with your GP. Medical confidentiality is such that other people will know you are 'on pills' only if you choose to tell them.

Try asking yourself what prompts you to 'go it alone'. Instead of making this a snap decision, consider whether you may feel secretly ashamed of being 'stupidly' unable to cope, or whether you are convinced that, being weak, wicked and justifiably unwanted, you are just not worth the bother? You will understand more about how counterproductive your thoughts can be when you are depressed after you've read the chapter on cognitive therapy (*see page 84*).

People who choose to fight depression alone sometimes say that at least they are not papering over the cracks – in other words, blurring their awareness of and ability to deal with personal issues by falsely boosting their mood. This is a valid point, but it's equally true that feeling better in body, mind and spirit, with improved motivation and mental energy, sounder sleep, healthier appetite and a reawakened interest in your everyday affairs, empowers you to deal with, rather than succumb to, stress triggers, and hopefully keep going when your world is falling apart.

'I'm scared of the side effects'

Like all drugs, antidepressants can cause side effects, most of which are trivial and wear off within two to three weeks of starting the course. Some of these effects have, however, been blown out of proportion or misreported, and it's essential to distinguish fact from fiction. Firstly, if you fear that antidepressants will make you ill because many types of medication do disagree with you, then your GP, who knows your medical history, can recommend one that is likely to suit you, and later change it to another if need be.

Approximately 60 per cent of sufferers have their depression relieved by their first course of treatment; around 80 per cent when unsuitable 'starter' choices are discarded in favour of a substitute. The most common reason for failure of anti-depressant therapy in general practice is insufficient medication – either because the doses are too low, or because the patient does not take them for long enough. Many people feel that this reflects the GP's desire to please their patients, without giving enough thought to the likely outcome. In bending over backwards to compromise between a perceived need for the patient to take the medication and the patient's unwillingness so to do, the doctor ameliorates the situation by 'soft' prescribing – too little of a drug for too short a time. By textbook standards this is bad medicine, but in an imperfect world it is often better to get a patient to agree to take *some* of a medication that they need, rather than none at all.

If you're remembering side effects reported by a friend on antidepressants, remember that no drug suits every person. How you and I respond to the same dose of a medication prescribed for the same complaint is influenced by our general health, our age, our state of mind and any other medicines we may be taking.

You may have heard horror stories during the 1990s when Prozac (fluoxetine) was reported to be 'inciting patients to murder or suicide', or Seroxat to be 'making patients suicidal'. The following information might help you make up your mind about these drugs. Studies have concluded that Prozac can release inhibitions in certain people, liberating aggressive urges that they had hitherto repressed. It is rarely prescribed nowadays for anyone with known aggressive tendencies; but it does have the advantage of lifting a low mood more quickly than other antidepressants of this class, often within five to seven days. It's also an effective appetite suppressant, and therefore often suits overweight depressed people who tend to comfort eat. Additionally, it is excellent at combating the depressive symptom of daytime drowsiness.

As for Seroxat – I was one of the unlucky ones who needed hospital admission to cope with the fallout of its being stopped abruptly. My GP was at fault but, to be fair, the drug had not been around for long, and less was known about the effects of its sudden withdrawal. The experience was upsetting at the time, but small doses soon put matters right and I suffered no lasting problems. It is an effective antidepressant, and I have prescribed it a number of times since then.

TYPES OF ANTIDEPRESSANT

Here are descriptions of the main types of antidepressant, together with the information you will need if you're going to take them.

Antidepressants work in various ways, but their common objective is to increase the quantities of serotonin, noradrenaline and dopamine in the brain, and/or improve their efficiency at the receptor sites (*see page 39*). A typical example is the action of the SSRIs (*see below*) in promoting serotonin activity, which they accomplish by interfering with an enzyme that destroys serotonin in the synaptic fluid during the transmission of a 'brain message'. This leaves active serotonin molecules in the fluid for longer, with increased chances of enhancing a low mood.

The mood-lifting effects of most antidepressants become apparent after ten to fourteen days (although as mentioned before, Prozac works more quickly), and increase until the end of the third week. However, they often relieve insomnia and other physical symptoms, such as lethargy, fatigue and appetite problems, within a few days of starting.

Selective serotonin reuptake inhibitors (SSRIs)

These were introduced into the UK in the late 1980s and early 1990s. They are many doctors' drugs of first choice for relieving depression (and obsessional disorders). They are safer than the tricyclics (*see below*) because, in overdose, they are less likely to cause serious heart disturbances. They also produce fewer of the so-called antimuscarinic side effects – that is, a dry mouth, blurred vision, drowsiness, constipation and difficulty in urinating.

Commonly prescribed SSRIs, besides those already mentioned, include venlafaxine (Efexor), fluvoxamine (Faverin) and citalopram (Cipromil). Their side effects may include nausea and vomiting, stomach ache, diarrhoea or constipation, appetite disturbances and rashes.

Tricyclics

Named after their molecular structure, the tricyclics have been around for nearly half a century, during which time the original drugs have been added to and improved. They are the antidepressants of choice for the type of depression that seems to arise for no identifiable reason (*see* endogenous depression *page 17*), especially when the person is experiencing serious problems with appetite loss and sleep disturbances.

Improved sleep is usually the first benefit of taking these drugs to be noticed, particularly when tricyclics with noted sedative effects are prescribed, such as amitriptyline (Triptafen), clomipramine (Anafranil) and doxepin (Sinequan). Of course, they are also more likely to cause daytime drowsiness, and when this needs to be avoided, tricyclics such as imipramine (Tofranil), lofepramine (Gamanil) and nortriptyline (Motival) are normally selected.

Tricyclics are usually avoided – or prescribed with great caution – in patients with heart disease because they can interfere with the electrical impulses that maintain a normal heartbeat, and in some patients with epilepsy because they have been known to cause convulsions. They also give rise to the muscarinic side effects already mentioned above.

Monoamine oxidase inhibitors (MAOIs)

These include phenelzine (Nardil), isocarboxazid and tranylcypromine. They tend to be prescribed far less often than the other two antidepressant groups, mainly because of the danger of interactions between them and other drugs and certain foods.

MAOIs take up to three weeks to produce their full benefits (and occasionally a further fortnight), but studies show that they are well worth trying when other antidepressants have failed because some people improve dramatically on them. They work by inhibiting an enzyme, monoamine oxidase, which destroys the mood-benefiting brain neurotransmitters. When the good mood chemicals are at a low level, we feel depressed. Abolishing the action of monoamine oxidase, the chemical that destroys them, permits dopamine, serotonin and noradrenaline to accumulate, raising the mood and fighting depression symptoms.

The problem with the MAOIs is that they also interfere with the way the body handles amine compounds found in many cold and decongestant medicines, which can cause agonising headache and dangerously high blood pressure if the two are taken in conjunction. Eating foods rich in the amino acid tyramine produces similar results – the so-called 'cheese effect'. Foods to avoid if you are taking an MAOI include pickled herrings, chocolate, broad bean pods, mature cheese, fermented soya bean extract (soy sauce), and meat and yeast extracts such as Oxo, Marmite, Vegemite and Bovril. Game and all foods that have gone off, especially fish, meat, offal and poultry, are hazardous, as may be alcohol and dealcoholised drinks.

The danger of food and drug interactions persists for about two weeks after a course of MAOIs finishes. Treatment with other antidepressants should not be started for a fortnight afterwards, or three weeks if the new drug is the tricyclic clomipramine or imipramine.

Electric shock treatment

Electroconvulsive therapy (ECT) is a type of antidepressant because it acts similarly to the drugs described above, by raising serotonin and other mood neurotransmitter levels. You could come across it if you are very severely depressed, so it may help you to know a little about it. Essentially, electrical activity in the form of waves is present in the brain throughout life, and it can be studied on an electroencephalograph. This is a tracing of brain-wave patterns picked up (painlessly) by electrodes running from various parts of the cranium to a recording machine. Disturbances such as those that occur in epilepsy, for example, can be detected from irregularities in the wave pattern.

Shock therapy developed following the observation by doctors that patients with epilepsy and depression tend to be less depressed after they have had a seizure. It dawned on the doctors that improvements in depressive symptoms may be brought about in people who did not suffer from epilepsy if a current were applied to their heads to induce a small convulsion. The treatment worked in the early twentieth century and it continues to work today, although many people consider it barbaric.

In fact, the original, somewhat primitive method of seizure induction has undergone many refinements, and it is much safer now than it was even ten years ago – partly because of improved immediate aftercare. In the early days, the patient was conscious throughout the procedure. Nowadays, the patient receives a short-acting general anaesthetic to send them to sleep and a muscle relaxant to minimise the physical seizure and prevent injury. A small current is passed through their brain via electrodes placed on their temples, and the whole treatment is over in a few minutes. Most people are admitted to hospital during the treatment course, although it is possible to receive ECT as an outpatient. The patient's progress is carefully monitored between treatments, which are normally given twice weekly for between six and twelve sessions.

ECT does not work for everyone, but it can bring about the most dramatic improvement and can certainly save the lives of people who are too sick to respond to antidepressant drugs. It might be recommended as an emergency treatment for someone who is severely suicidal, for instance, or who is not eating or drinking. How ECT achieves its results is not entirely understood, but it is believed to boost the quantities and activity of dopamine, noradrenaline and serotonin in the brain. It's common to wake with a mild headache and remember little of what has happened on the day of the treatment before the anaesthetic, but the majority of people who require (and are given) ECT undoubtedly benefit.

SPECIFIC TYPES OF DEPRESSION

Some types of depression have unique features or triggers and occasionally require idiosyncratic treatment instead of, or in addition to, antidepressant drugs. Here I mention post-natal depression, manic depression, drug- and alcohol-induced depression, and SAD (seasonal affective disorder) as examples.

Post-natal depression

Feeling sad or moody a day or so after having a baby is a healthy, natural experience for nearly 50 per cent of all new mothers. If you have experienced it yourself, you may remember the mixed emotions that crowd in at that time – joy and relief that the pregnancy is safely over, delight in your new offspring, pleasure in the happiness of your partner, family and friends and, if it's a first child, the wonder of really being a mother.

At the same time, you are probably exhausted, sore, naturally still overweight and anxious about how you will manage and care for your new arrival. Your body is flooding with hormones, which in turn affect your mood and stamina. Mood swings, feeling elated one minute and sad, irritable and tearful the next, are all part of the baby blues, which tend to come on within the first week, especially on the fourth day, after your delivery. They usually pass within a couple of days with ample rest, and reassurance and support from those around you.

In nearly all respects, baby blues differ from post-natal depressive illness, which affects between 10 and 15 per cent of all women for two weeks or longer. As in the case of 'ordinary' depression, the symptoms can be mild, moderate or severe, and occur in the weeks and months after the birth, with the more serious variety usually, although not always, starting during the first four weeks. Nearly one in two women who develop post-natal depression need treatment – without which the illness can persist for months.

While the hormonal changes that take place after childbirth are doubtless partly responsible, the other triggers are much the same as those for non-natal depressive illness. Of particular importance are the fears we may entertain of inadequacy – being a bad mother and failing to live up to our own or other people's expectations. The absence of a supportive partner, and having had depression in the past, also make post-natal depression more likely. A course of antidepressant treatment combined with supportive counselling or cognitive therapy usually brings good results.

For the sake of completion, I also describe puerperal psychosis (psychotic illness following childbirth) because it is sometimes confused with post-natal depression, although it is really beyond the scope of this book. Puerperal psychosis is a severe mental illness experienced by about one in 500 new mothers, usually starting within the first two weeks of having a baby. Some women who develop it have had a psychotic illness in the past, or close family members who have had it. This illness is equally distressing for the sufferer and her loved ones. The symptoms are generally acute and frequently frightening, with the affected person becoming severely confused and disorientated, and showing mood swings, abnormal behaviour and thoughts, and the hallmarks of psychosis – false beliefs (delusions) and hallucinations (seeing, hearing and smelling things that are not there).

The following case history of Renee illustrates how disturbing post-natal depression can be. She was twenty-seven when I saw her during a hospital ward round after she had been admitted with deep depression and thoughts of killing herself and her baby. This is what she told me.

CASE HISTORY: RENEE

I was twenty-three when I married Fred. We met in the park while walking our dogs. He was two years older than me, and a policeman. I had recently broken off my engagement to my childhood sweetheart, and was fancy-free – not yet looking for another rela-tionship, but of course we can't plan these things . . .

Fred and I hit it off from the start. We went out for only nine months before he proposed, and we got officially engaged the follow-ing Christmas. I was so happy. I was working as a dispenser in our local general hospital, and Fred had applied to train as a dog handler. We bought a little cottage in the village with roses around the door, and settled down blissfully to married life. We'd planned to have at least three years to ourselves before starting a family, but we had an accident with a condom one night and three weeks later I found I was pregnant. We were a bit taken aback at first, but soon we both felt delighted at the prospect of becoming parents.

Then, two days after my sixteen-week scan, which was perfectly normal, I started to bleed heavily and we lost our baby two days later. We were devastated, of course, but I suppose we hadn't had time to relate too closely to our unborn child, and I got over it by pretending to myself that I'd just had a heavy period rather than a miscarriage. Fred was wonderful – he asked me if I wanted to try for a baby again straight away. This is what we did.

My pregnancy was normal throughout and Sarah was born on the expected date, after only five hours' labour. We were simply over the moon. I had no baby blues to speak of. I just felt very tired and a bit moody at the end of the first week. But a fortnight into my life as a first-time mum, the world crashed down around my ears.

I woke up one morning and couldn't stop crying. I snapped at Fred, screamed at Sarah, and sat weeping in the lounge all day, surrounded by nappies, baby clothes, and dirty cups and plates from the night before when we'd had guests. All this was completely out of character, yet it went on for over a fortnight – Fred was on night duty and couldn't offer much practical help, but he was very worried about me. Then my mum came round unexpectedly. She took one look at me and rang the doctor. The fact is she recognised the symptoms of post-natal depression because she had had it after my two elder sisters were born.

I was rude and unco-operative when the doctor called – again quite out of character. But she managed to persuade me to let Sarah go to Mum, and to spend a few days in the psychiatric ward of a hospital some distance away (that is, not the one where I had worked). While there, I went completely to pieces for a few days, and felt I wanted to end it all. But the antidepressant I was put on ensured some sound sleep and the counselling helped me to explore a stress factor I hadn't taken into account – the grief I had never expressed at losing our first child. I felt a million times better when I was discharged after ten days, and haven't looked back since.

A tendency to suffer from post-natal depression may or may not be inherited; but having a close relative who was affected may have increased the chances of someone in Renee's position experiencing it – partly for genetic reasons, and partly due to the sort of lifestyle common to that family. The latter did not seem relevant to Renee, but generally speaking, living under extremely crowded, stressful conditions (for instance) with younger family members bringing up their babies in the same environment as that of their parents, would increase the risks of successive generations of mothers experiencing this illness.

Manic depression, or bipolar affective disorder

Also known as bipolar depression (BD), manic depression is a complex illness featuring pronounced mood swings. The highs and lows we nearly all experience – feeling sad one minute and on top of the world the next – are transformed by BD into clinical depression and an elated state called mania. The depression shares the sadness, loss of pleasure, poor self-esteem and other features already described for the illness, while the mania is marked by a high-pitched euphoria entirely out of proportion with the person's circumstances. Sufferers often come over as – and have described feeling – enormously powerful and self-important, and frequently talk expansively about grand or daring plans and ideas that they would certainly never contemplate when well. Their energy appears unbounded, their speech is loud and rapid, and they typically flit from one activity or topic to the next, attacking it with gusto before dropping it for another.

Subjectively, the manic phase of BD brings a sense of intense well-being, but even this has its drawbacks, as does the energy surge that interferes with sleep and can lead to physical and mental collapse and exhaustion. Some sufferers are vexed, on coming out of a manic phase, at their uninhibited, often impulsive, behaviour. Cruelly, mania can convert a quiet, polite, even-tempered friend or relation into a walking embarrassment who talks to, or shouts at, all and sundry, quickly becomes agitated or truculent, and makes risqué suggestions to complete strangers.

Christina was thirty-one when she was admitted to hospital for the first time with symptoms of mania. I took over her treatment after her discharge, and she told me her story.

CASE HISTORY: CHRISTINA

I suffered from depression as a teenager, but when Mum took me to the doctor he said it was premenstrual tension and put me on the Pill. I left school at sixteen, had various jobs as a barmaid and cleaner, then married my childhood sweetheart Beni when we were both nineteen. I managed to stay free of depression for a year or two, then the kids started arriving, Beni lost his job and I got stressed out.

I was very depressed after the birth of our third child Scott, who was born with Down's syndrome. We were living in a dilapidated Housing Association flat near gasworks and railway lines, and existed on benefits. Then, when I was expecting Sheena, Beni went off with a mate of mine and I got so depressed that the kids had to go into care. My doctor prescribed an antidepressant, but I didn't take it. I don't believe in taking drugs.

I got better on my own, and stayed more or less OK until a year ago, when I started to get funny moods. It's ironic – life was just picking up for us, I was back in a barmaid's job and as a cleaner at Tescos after hours, and I had started seeing Wayne, my best mate's brother. Then my sister died suddenly – she was run over by a bus – and that was a terrible shock. I got depressed and Wayne had just persuaded me to go to the doctor, when suddenly I felt completely different – marvellous, never felt like it before in my life. I felt so strong and powerful, I was always raring to go, never went to sleep for at least two weeks and felt excited about anything and everything.

'Wayne tried to tell me that I needed medical help but I thought he was mad! I would get very irritable with him and shout and scream and throw things one minute, then make up the next. I remember singing at the top of my voice while I was hoovering at 2 am, with the TV and CD player both on max. When my neighbours complained, I told them where to go! Usually I am careful with money, but I was sure I had thousands in the bank, and took my bit of plastic on a spending spree. I got through more than two thousand pounds in an afternoon, on clothes I didn't really like and food the kids wouldn't touch. They got fed up with their mum, and even Wayne got the hump – said he couldn't cope. But I didn't care – until the hallucinations started.

I saw strangers in the street bowing and curtseying to me, which reminded me that I was Prince Philip's cousin. Then I started to hear messages in Morse code on the radio from aliens, saying they'd chosen me to save the world. Goodness knows what I would have done if my eldest son hadn't contacted Wayne, who went round and told my doctor what was happening. When he arrived, he tried to get me to go into hospital. I was mad at him, and shouted and swore. But he decided I needed to go in under a section, and this was arranged between him, the psychiatrist and a social worker.

> They had a job getting me in the ambulance, and keeping me on the ward for the first few days. But the tablets started to work and I settled down. I was in hospital for five weeks, and go back every two months to see the consultant. I'm on lithium and an antidepressant, and there are a few side effects – shakiness, drowsiness and I've gained a bit of weight – but I am miles better and more stable. In fact, I may not even get any further mood bouts if I stay on the tablets and don't get too stressed. At least Wayne and I are back together again, and I'm grateful for that.

Psychotic symptoms can occur in severe BD, causing a loss of contact with reality. The sufferer experiences delusions or false beliefs, and hallucinations, which is seeing and hearing things that are not really there, as Christina did. Both the delusions and the hallucinations tend to be in keeping with the person's euphoria and sense of great self-importance. Delusions of grandeur are in fact a characteristic feature of BD, convincing the sufferer that they have, for example, won the National Lottery or the Eurovision Song Contest, or that they are a member of the Royal Family.

Around one in a hundred people in the UK are thought to suffer from BD at some time in their lives. It tends to run in families, and researchers are trying to identify the genes involved. If you are affected, you may have one or two bouts of illness only, or go on to experience repeated episodes of depression or mania. Either phase can be triggered by stressful life events, and if you can anticipate and avoid these wherever possible and seek help when they occur, you can reduce the risks of a relapse.

The depressive phases of BD are treated with antidepressants and psychotherapy, like other depression. Bouts of mania are usually treated with antipsychotic medication such as chlorpromazine (Largactil) or haloperidol (Serenace, Haldol), whose side effects of stiffness, shakiness, dry mouth and constipation can be relieved with other medication.

Admission to hospital is sometimes needed for severe depressive or manic bouts.

Mood-stabilising drugs, such as lithium, are often prescribed when the illness is acute to help prevent relapses. Lithium treatment has to be monitored with regular blood tests to ensure that the lithium level is high enough to be beneficial but not so high as to cause symptoms of toxicity. Side effects can include shakiness, thirst, weight gain and passing more urine than usual, while toxicity causes staggering, vomiting and slurred speech. Should you experience these last mentioned, you should contact your doctor at once.

Drug- and alcohol-induced depression

This is a huge topic to which I cannot hope to do justice in this book, but if you drink alcohol or use street drugs, it's important to be clear about the links between these substances and depression. You are particularly at risk if there's a family history of depressive illness, although these substances in themselves – regardless of inherited traits and other lifestyle risk factors – can lead to severe depression.

Alcohol and depression

Everyone who has experienced a hangover knows how low it makes you feel; but are you also aware that heavy drinking itself can trigger depressive illness? In fact, while most regular drinkers drown their sorrows once in a while in their favourite tipple, *depression is more often the outcome than the cause* of alcohol misuse.

Guidelines for healthy drinking recommend up to twenty-one units a week for men and up to fourteen for women, with one or two alcohol-free days every week, and no more than four units per day for men and three for women. The difference between men's and women's safety limits is due to the fact that women's bodies contain more fat than men's, and because they metabolise alcohol less efficiently.

One unit is the alcohol present in a standard measure of spirits, half a pint of normal-strength beer or lager, 125 ml of 9 per cent wine, or a single shot of liqueur or measure of sherry, vermouth or similar fortified wine. Some vintners and breweries are starting to include information on alcohol units on labels and packaging. This trend should prove very helpful, because it is only too easy to 'count' a half pint of lager, say, or a 'medium' glass of wine as one unit, without having a clear idea of how much alcohol the drink contains.

Mostly, you may stick to the guidelines, but it is only too easy to underestimate how much you're drinking, especially when your mood is low, or you're drinking alone or at a friend's home, where measures are generally much bigger.

Alcohol appears to cheer us up because it replaces shyness with temporary self-confidence and relieves acute anxiety or grief – for a while. But even binge drinkers know this is not the answer. Problems are harder, not simpler, to face and sort out the next day, and the drinking quickly becomes habitual – causing dependence and requiring ever larger amounts to provide the same effect.

Alcohol's action on the brain is wholly depressant. It deadens our 'higher senses', which warn us when to keep our mouths shut. Our released inhibitions can make us over-confident and brash, or channel pent-up aggression into torrents of abuse. Alcohol can also bring powerful feelings of self-loathing to the surface, bringing on depression and suicidal thoughts. Heavy drinking adversely affects the brain's mood chemicals, and can cause structural changes evident on a CT brain scan in the frontal lobes, which control our socially useful inhibitions.

When heavy drinking and depression coincide, cutting down or cutting out alcohol can relieve the depression and improve mental and physical health generally. If you find this difficult, you should see your doctor or contact the national Alcohol Line or Alcoholics Anonymous (*see page 178*) for advice and support. Any residual depression can then be treated with an antidepressant and/or psychotherapy. The following case history illustrates how easily we can overlook the link between drinking and depression.

CASE HISTORY: PAUL

Paul was fifty-six when he first suffered from depression, and described his history to me as follows.

'I had never suffered from depression in my life before my wife died. We had celebrated our silver wedding anniversary the year before, and we both had retirement plans for the near future. Then, while we were away in Greece in May 2001, Meg started to feel ill and I took her to a local doctor.

'We thought she just had a tummy bug but, after tests and a scan, the doctor advised us to return home and see our family doctor urgently. She wouldn't be drawn on the diagnosis, which I suppose was fair, considering. Meg was found to have in-operable cancer of the ovary, and although our hopes were raised that chemotherapy and radiotherapy might help, they brought her only temporary relief. Meg died ten months to the day from our flight home from Athens.

'To say I was devastated doesn't begin to reveal how I felt. It had all happened so quickly that I found it difficult, even at the funeral, to accept that Meg had really gone. My best mate (he'd been best man at our wedding) came home with me for the night, and we got absolutely plastered. I've always enjoyed a drink, but Meg was teetotal and I rarely indulged. I felt horrible the next day, but all I could do was count the hours until 6 pm when I could have another drink. All I could clearly remember was the wonderful floating feeling, and the relief being drunk had given me.

'By the end of the first week I was drinking at lunchtime, and by the end of a month I was having Scotch and soda first thing. It was a twilight world – sickness every morning, sweaty, restless nights with agonising calf cramp and terrifying dreams. Then, next day, the ever available, dependable crutch, which let me cry and scream in pain, break things or just quietly relive a million memories of our life together.

'It didn't last, of course. When the time came to return to work, I couldn't face it. I got a doctor's sick note and stayed at home, but by now I was weeping on and off all day and gradually falling apart. I couldn't cope with the paperwork following Meg's death, the household bills, having the car serviced, even walking the dog. I was sleeping badly, losing weight, hating myself for not coping and eventually dwelling on suicide.

'That is when I went to see my doctor. She took a full case history including any emotional disorders (none) and how much I was drinking. She diagnosed depression triggered by bereavement and heavy drinking, and warned me that binge drinking increases the risks of a stroke. She told me to stop the booze, and I found I needed help. I started to attend AA meetings, and by the time of my next doctor's appointment, my mood was starting to improve. I've stayed off alcohol for a year now, and shan't drink again. An antidepressant and bereavement counselling were both very useful.'

Cannabis and depression

Clear links have been established between the use of cannabis and depression. Two studies appearing in the *British Medical Journal* in November 2002 demonstrated the risks of heavy or frequent use. The first study, by an Australian research team, monitored 1,600 teenage girls over a seven-year period. The girls who used the drug every day were five times more likely than non-users to suffer from depression and anxiety. Once-a-week users were twice as likely to become depressed as non-users.

The second study, by a research team in Sweden, involved 50,000 men, some of whom had smoked cannabis in the late 1960s. It confirmed previous research suggesting that cannabis can increase the risks of developing depression. Those with a history of cannabis use were also 30 per cent more likely to have developed schizophrenia than those without such a history. This probably results from a combination of factors: an inherent brain chemical defect waiting to be sparked into a schizophrenic experience, and the psychosis-inducing effects of the chemicals present in cannabis itself.

Studies have also shown that ecstasy, cocaine and amphetamines increase the risks of depression, and most narcotic addicts show signs of clinical depression when withdrawing from heroin, methadone, morphine and other such drugs. You can obtain further advice on drug problems from your doctor, Narcotics Anonymous (*see page 180*) and other national help lines.

Seasonal affective disorder (SAD)

If your depression regularly starts in the autumn or early winter and disappears in the spring, the chances are that you are suffering from SAD. 'Affective' refers to mood, and SAD is thought to be triggered by a lack of exposure to daylight. It affects around one in twenty people, and is more common in northern countries where winter days are short, than in countries where they are longer. People between the ages of sixteen and forty are most at risk of SAD, and women are three times likelier than men to suffer from it.

The symptoms are similar to those of the more common depression, and include feeling low and tired, with little energy and poor sex drive. Some people also suffer from disturbed sleep, and eat significantly more or less than usual. The usual triggers also apply: difficult relationships, money worries, working too hard or too long, family demands and little time for oneself all provide the stress that can help to precipitate SAD.

Signs of SAD usually disappear spontaneously (other factors being equal) in spring when the days noticeably lengthen. You can help to minimise the risk by getting out of the house as often as possible – even an overcast day provides exposure to natural light, and exercise in the fresh air helps to boost the brain's good mood chemicals. Rest, relaxation and other stress-beating measures are also useful. Your doctor may recommend an antidepressant and some psychotherapy if your SAD symptoms persist.

One useful natural treatment I recommend is phototherapy. Light boxes and dawn simulators (and other similar devices) have been designed to supplement exposure to natural daylight. They can be used at home or at work, and can be plugged into a household electrical socket like an ordinary lamp (*see page 179* for further information).

Next, though, we take a look at the 'Talking Treatment'.

CHAPTER 5

The Talking Treatment

Besides prescribing an antidepressant, your doctor may suggest a course of psychotherapy – and again, I must urge you to see your doctor if you believe you are depressed and need help. As I mentioned earlier, medication and psychotherapy in combination are generally most effective at relieving depression. The type of psychotherapy known as cognitive behavioural therapy, or CBT, is especially helpful. Other forms of psychotherapy can sometimes help and, since there is a good deal of misunderstanding about the 'talking treatments', it's helpful to understand a few general facts about them, and what actually happens during treatment.

Psychotherapy comes in many forms, but they all share the goal of helping people deal more successfully with emotional problems, relationship difficulties, stress and unhelpful thinking patterns, which are discussed further in this chapter. They all involve some kind of dialogue between the patient (or client), and the person carrying out the treatment, the therapist. In certain instances, the patient and the therapist may also share an activity relating to the patient's problem; an experimental trip to the supermarket, for instance, for someone with agoraphobia (fear of crowds and open spaces), which often triggers depression in sufferers.

Psychotherapy is often called the 'talking treatment', but a better name for it would be the 'talking–listening treatment'. Generally, the patient talks more than the therapist, and one of the latter's skills lies in listening and hearing what the patient is saying. However, listening and understanding on both sides are fundamental to psychotherapy's success. Psychodynamic psychotherapy, for instance, which approaches the patient's personal and emotional problems from a psycho-analytical standpoint, demands a particular ability 'to read between the lines' of a patient's remarks, because what the patient hints at or leaves unsaid may be even more signifi-cant than what he or she reveals. To an extent, this is true of all psychotherapy, but the analytical approach (which takes much longer) tends to scrutinise the latent meaning of the patient's remarks more than most.

Psychotherapy is no easy option – talking to a stranger about personal problems may seem strange at first, and it can take several sessions for communication to flow freely. The rela-tionship between the patient and therapist is important. Successful therapy involves hard work and the mutual effort of both participants. Therapists, of course, are trained to relate to patients of all types; and patients, in the main, want to get better. Occasionally, though, through no fault of either, empathy fails to develop. Both patient and therapist are usually aware, even in the early stages, that they are not destined to get on. The best solution in these circumstances is for the patient to find, or to be referred to, another therapist.

WHAT ACTUALLY HAPPENS DURING PSYCHOTHERAPY?

A course of psychotherapy usually involves regular meetings at the same time, same place every week or fortnight. Generally the length of the treatment will be agreed between you, the patient, and the therapist shortly after starting.

Matters discussed and emotions expressed are nearly always confidential, but if for some reason the GP or psychiatrist who referred you needed to be kept in the picture, the information would only be shared with your knowledge and consent.

In individual psychotherapy, you could expect to talk to a therapist alone in a quiet room for fifty to sixty minutes at a time. This is not in the least alarming – there is nearly always a receptionist or secretary to let you in, and a quiet and private waiting room. If you haven't met the therapist before, then he or she will introduce themselves and make sure that you feel at ease.

The therapist may sit at a desk in order to take notes, or you may simply sit facing one another in comfortable armchairs. After a few minutes' social chat the therapist would gently prompt you to start talking about yourself, your feelings, and anything else relevant to your depression. Clients sometimes demur, and say they'd like to mention a topic but are not sure if it is important enough. There is an unwritten rule that anything the client feels inclined to mention has some bearing on their situation. So there is no strain whatever, and every encouragement for you to tell your story your way.

As a participant in group therapy, on the other hand, you would be one of several men and women, possibly with various backgrounds and problems and with similar experiences, all meeting and sharing personal difficulties with each another and with the therapist. It is usual for the therapist to lead, by suggesting a topic relevant to most clients. You may be encouraged to contribute, but you would never be forced to do so. Group sessions also tend to take place weekly, but often last longer than in individual therapy. Group therapy might suit you particularly well if you've experienced problems with isolation and a lack of confidence. It's a supportive environment confirming that you are *not* alone with your difficulties, and offering opportunities to help others – a great self-esteem booster, and a positive step for many towards lasting relief.

On the other hand, if you tend to feel threatened by groups and relate more easily to people on a one-to-one basis, group therapy is probably not for you. Your GP or hospital psychiatrist would take your feelings on this point into account and attempt to refer you to the most appropriate kind of therapy.

CONCERNS ABOUT PSYCHOTHERAPY

Psychotherapy isn't for everyone, but some depressed people do not feel able to find out whether it might in fact help them – feeling anxious, exhausted and isolated can be powerful deterrents to trying something new. An objection that comes up again and again relates to the discussion of personal problems with a stranger. While this might seem daunting, think back to occasions when you've got chatting to someone in a café or on a train, for example, and ended up talking about yourself. It's often easier to share worries with someone outside the picture, who has no preformed opinions and no axe to grind, than with close friends or family members who (with the best will in the world) inevitably have agendas of their own. Some of us are born listeners, and therapists, who are usually empathic and approachable, do put you at your ease.

Another worry is that the therapist might play mind games, try to dominate you or insist that you follow his or her advice. Ironically, it is the opposite experience that tends to cause most dismay in the long run. We may boldly go down the independence route, saying that we'll handle our depression alone, but depression makes us emotionally frail, indecisive and poor at coping, with learned helplessness and a need to be comforted. Some patients long to be protected, nurtured and told what to do, but this is no more the therapist's role than is playing God or laying down the law.

Strict ethical guidelines are laid down for therapists just as they are for doctors. Yet waking from the cosy, confiding atmosphere that can build up during treatment sessions, to the realisation that the psychotherapist's function is to help you help yourself, is sometimes painful. Essentially, whatever type of psychotherapy you go in for, the fundamental truth remains that your therapist never truly becomes your friend. You may invite them into the hidden recesses of your secret soul, but ethically they remain detached, with a job to do on your behalf.

A third worry is 'that it would not do any good'. We saw in Chapter 2 how unburdening ourselves literally lifts weight from our minds, and can powerfully boost a depressed mood. If talking to strangers, friends or family can be helpful, talking to a trained professional can achieve much more. My best advice is at least to give it a try.

FINDING A PSYCHOTHERAPIST

Your GP or a psychiatrist can refer you to a local qualified psychotherapist. A therapist may be a psychotherapist pure and simple, a psychologist or other mental health professional such as a community psychiatric nurse (CPN), or a social worker who has been trained in psychotherapy. You can also find one for yourself through personal recommendation or by looking in the Yellow Pages. Don't be afraid to ask them about their qualifications, and whether they offer treatment specifically for depression. (See the Resources section on page 178 for more details about finding a psychotherapist.)

THREE TYPES OF PSYCHOTHERAPY

Here are descriptions of how three of the most common types of psychotherapy work.

Psychodynamic (or analytical) treatments

These focus on our feelings for others, especially family members and others close to us. They work from the standpoint that how we see and relate to the world as adolescents and adults results from our relationship experiences as babies and children; early disturbances tend to bring relationship problems later on. The treatment involves discussing such past experiences and how they may have led to current problems.

Understanding the connections between past and present can allow us to choose what happens in future. It might suit you if your depression seems to be due (at least in part) to previous trauma, especially those of childhood. You may be depressed and have difficulties in personal relationships, for example, after being bullied at school – even if this occurred many years ago. Treatment is relatively short for specific difficulties, but can go on for months for more involved problems. Sessions for individuals or couples are usually offered weekly.

Psychodynamic or analytical therapy tends to appeal to people who prefer to trace the origins of their problems, rather than apply psychological techniques for dispelling their symptoms. However, most patients tend to be treated privately, analytic work tends to be expensive and the longer it persists, the harder it can be to relinquish your relationship with the analyst when your treatment comes to an end.

If you are unsure about whether this treatment would be right for you, ask your GP or psychiatrist's opinion about your suitability for analysis, or at least discuss the matter fully with an analytical therapist of your choice before embarking upon a course of treatment.

Counselling

This is a general term for talking over emotional and relationship problems with a trained therapist or counsellor. At its simplest it is suitable for people with essentially healthy personalities, when it comprises weekly sessions over a relatively short period, in which the counsellor listens empathically and helps the patient to tackle a current crisis such as bereavement or divorce.

Some counsellors with more specialised training can help with more complex problems. Bereavement, rape, drugs and alcohol, childhood abuse, post-traumatic stress and relationship counselling are among their specialities. Counsellors are in the main relatively easily accessible through medical practitioner referrals, and play an invaluable role in the day-to-day management of emotional problems in the community.

There is really nothing intimidating about psychotherapy, but 'going for counselling' does sound simpler and more reassuring, and many depressed people who didn't feel comfortable seeing a psychotherapist finally see a counsellor and reap great benefit.

Cognitive behavioural therapy (CBT)

This is an amalgamation of behavioural therapy, which aims to change behaviour patterns that contribute to our depression (or other problems), and cognitive therapy, which tries to change how we think. On the surface, changing how we think may sound sinister; but far from being a form of mind control, cognitive therapy targets only those thinking patterns, such as automatic thoughts (*see page 92*), that predispose us to depression and impair our coping skills.

Like psychodynamic psychotherapy, cognitive work encourages us to study our thoughts and to leave behind destructive thinking patterns. But it generates a less intense, more supportive liaison with the therapist than does the psychodynamic approach, and focuses less on past experiences than on the present and future – that is, it spotlights the practical aspects of a current problem, rather than childhood experiences that may have contributed to it. Cognitive therapy has an excellent record in treating depression.

Behavioural therapy can help to protect us from depression

by teaching us how to reduce anxiety and how to overcome personal stress factors such as shopping, socialising, coping with crowds and driving in heavy traffic. Patients are often asked to keep diaries of their experiences between treatment sessions, and to practise new skills, for example having a cup of coffee in a restaurant when their chief fear is of fainting or of making a fool of themselves in public. Behavioural techniques may also relieve anxiety-driven complaints such as panic attacks, phobias, sexual problems and obsessive-compulsive disorder. These can co-exist with clinical depression although they are not an essential aspect of it, and many good books have been written about them for you to read if you wish.

The aims of CBT are to teach problem-solving strategies for coping, and for overcoming irrational fears. It was first developed in the United States from learning theory around the middle of the twentieth century by Aaron Beck, a medical doctor, psychiatrist and analyst who found analysis too slow, and based his treatment on the notion that our thoughts create our moods.

Parallels can be drawn between the cognitive approach to emotional problems and the stoic philosophy introduced by the Roman thinker Epictetus, who taught that we are not disturbed by circumstances and the things around us, but by how we view them. Every one of us has an inherent tendency to think negative thoughts when challenged. If we can accept this, we can learn to challenge destructive thoughts as they arise, and replace them with realistic alternatives.

CBT is a large subject, with which I cannot deal fully within the scope of this book. In this chapter I illustrate some of its pertinent points. I suggest that CBT is surely the form of therapy to go for if, firstly, you have a choice and, secondly, you are more interested in discovering ways of becoming depression-free in future than in identifying possible triggers from the past. Bear in mind that, as noted previously, CBT combined with antidepressant medication is also the most successful treatment on record for depression.

AUTOMATIC THOUGHTS

A typical example of negative, depression-provoking thinking was provided in Chapter 1: you imagine yourself going to meet a lover/close friend at the station and them failing to appear (*see page 21*). Automatic thoughts surface as inexorably as those wretched ads for genital enlargement or low-interest loans that pop up onto the screen when one is searching the Internet for one's local Tesco, for example, or a film review. One destructive thought after another comes crashing down and, although you may not be aware of a cause-and-effect sequence of ideas, your emotions soon become plain – you feel steadily worse, without always being sure why.

Negative thoughts of this type inevitably cascade, spiralling you into emotional imbalance and, ultimately, depression. The end result invariably casts long shadows over your self-esteem and coping ability, and even over how you feel about yourself physically.

Here is a possible end result of the fantasy that our loved one was not on the promised train because he/she has gone off with someone else:

- 'Of course he/she has better things to do. Why should they be interested in *me?*'
- 'No one *could* be interested in me for long – I am so stupid and boring.'
- 'I'm not very attractive either – what's the point of hoping for a good relationship?'
- 'Everyone else can find someone but me. I am useless – I may as well stop trying.'
- 'I'll always be alone, laughed at, joked about.'
- 'I would be better off dead.'
- And so on.

The thing to do is to build in an effective brake. Notice how you are thinking in reaction to a specific situation, and be prepared for the next time the sequence strikes. Take the very next explanation/outcome of a challenging experience – say the reason for your friend failing to arrive at the station – and write it down. 'He/she was not on the train *because* their bus from home broke down/their mother became ill/they stopped to buy me a present/take an important telephone call and missed the train.' Try to think outwardly, that is in terms of real world events, not inwardly, referring everything back to yourself. Keep what you've written on a scrap of paper in your handbag or pocket, and get it out and read it whenever you are threatened again.

For a more organised approach, buy a small notebook – small enough to keep with you always – and write down the challenging (triggering) event (for example, him/her not being on the train), then the negative thoughts and emotions it triggered, followed by challenges to the negative thoughts. My therapist taught me to 'step outside myself' and become my own best friend. What would I say to someone thinking as I am thinking, as their closest friend? What positive, reasonable alternatives could I put forward to the negative assumptions they make?

Dare to examine the indictments levelled against yourself and your world by the negative thoughts, as though you were a defence counsel at the Old Bailey. Are the allegations born out by the evidence? Almost assuredly not! Could depression be clouding your 'friend's' – that is, your own – judgement? Yes, it certainly could. And, importantly, how have your friend's – that is, your – feelings changed after doing this exercise?

Logically, of course, if you weren't ultimately responsible for the event in question, the chances are that you are not responsible on other occasions. Work through this exercise repeatedly, as new situations arise. You will gradually come to see that you are not to blame for the chance experiences of others. You're not even responsible for them changing their minds about you (if they do). Only they are responsible for that.

DEALING WITH SPECIFIC FEARS

If we are really prone to negative thinking, we have to work at combating it constantly, which means recognising negative thoughts whenever they arise. CBT opens a window and lets in some sunshine upon the cobwebby thought patterns leading to a low mood. And while it does not dispel them for ever, it *does* provide us with ways of tackling them head on.

Dread of muddle

I can give you an up-to-the-minute example of negative thinking that is challenging me as I write. Yesterday I had my study fitted out with built-in furniture. It cost me far more than I had planned to spend, but I told myself that I would soon earn enough to fill the gaping hole in my bank account. I find money concerns particularly threatening, especially when I fear I may have acted impulsively and am likely to regret it later.

Now, although my new study is as lovely as I could have wished, I am surrounded, as I write, by a hopeless mess. I hate clutter and muddle, and my papers, books, writing notes, paper staplers, printer ink refills, mouse mat and correspondence are still strewn around my bedroom awaiting placement in their new homes. I need to work on this manuscript, but I am doing locum surgeries all day tomorrow, at a practice I have never before visited, a hundred miles from here. I feel that, at the same time as I am writing my book, I should be looking up tomorrow's route on the Internet *and* trying to get things straight at home. Meanwhile, I am worrying about one of my cats who seems unwell, my dog is begging for a walk and I am expecting a plumber to arrive at any minute to provide a quote for a bathroom shower.

Have you noticed anything about the words I have used so far – which were entirely spontaneous and unplanned? I have referred to my situation as 'threatening', 'a hopeless mess' and '(hated) clutter and muddle', and I have also accused myself of 'acting impulsively' (which I am doomed to 'regret'). It's clear that, in feeling driven to do several things at once, I am starting to panic in the face of 'uncontrollable stress'. Unsurprisingly, my mood, already at knee level, is dropping steadily into my boots.

My own particular way of challenging this and similar situations is to remind myself that, despite my impulsive nature, I've always managed difficult situations so far (thanks very much!), and to tell myself to calm down. I do feel (and always have felt) in danger of being swamped by muddle, so I ask myself whether any *real* danger lies in these unlovely heaps of paper and books? Of course it doesn't! I have nearly finished editing this chapter – that will be one load off my mind.

Secondly, I have planned an hour's walk with my new boyfriend for the early afternoon, and the inevitable climb up steep hills that this will entail will give me a chance to work off my pent-up frustration. I have only to locate my timesheet for locum surgeries I did last week, and to fax them off to my agency, who will then be able to pay me. And I have four hours left in the day to check the route to tomorrow's medical centre, plus all night (if I need it) to check the route on the Internet.

I am getting into a tizz about trivialities. I recognise that I am more than capable of dealing with them, and that I have survived far greater muddles in the past. My negative thoughts are scattered, and my spirits are starting to rise.

Health concerns

It's easy to get worked up about physical symptoms, and many people jump to conclusions that make them suffer unnecessarily. So here is a plan for coping with such situations worked out in full, dealing with a fear of cancer as it arises, that is before the test results are known. Suppose, for instance, that you have a breast lump, and that your doctor has told you that it is almost certainly benign. You've had a benign lump removed from that breast in the past, and the present one feels similar. You've been for a mammogram to set your mind at rest, although the doctor admitted this wasn't strictly necessary. Then you learn that you must wait a month for the result, and suddenly the worry is driving you crazy and you become convinced that it's cancer. You're facing what you perceive as uncontrollable stress. Next stop, depression.

Ask yourself whether you must endure a fortnight of hell, not eating, not sleeping, unable to work, always in tears? Should you resort to chain smoking, living on Valium or ringing up friends at all hours, seeking reassurance? Or should you befriend yourself, and meet your terror head on? The triggering event was the projected wait for the mammogram result on top of the confirmation of a breast lump, which unleashed negative thoughts about the outcome, and feelings of doom and terror you didn't realise you were capable of.

So . . . what are the actual facts of the case as they stand? Another breast lump much like the last one, which was benign, and which the doctor thinks is harmless, having given you a mammogram. Does having to wait for the result 'on top of everything else' *really* have to mean it's cancer? Pretty shaky grounds, aren't they, for reaching such a conclusion? Not one you'd let a friend jump to in similar circumstances. Do you really believe this cancer story, despite the non-existent evidence? Objectively, and on a scale of one to a hundred, how much faith do you have in these hasty conclusions now? How much of your original terror do you feel, after reviewing the situation? Ninety per cent? Fifty per cent? Ten per cent? Or in reality, hardly any – one to two per cent?

Hammer this improvement home by actually writing down what you would say to your best friend caught up in this drama. What positive points that she has forgotten in her storm of negative thoughts and emotions could you remind her of? How can you best challenge her biased slant on the subject?

How threatening do you feel the situation really is now that is has been freed of reactive fear? How much better do you feel now? Isn't it worth our repeating this exercise – based on rational argument, and not on automatic thoughts and feelings – as often as we can, to obtain credible relief? It's important to see, too, that we are not giving ourselves false hopes, or spinning ourselves a yarn to replace the initial bad fairy tale. By getting things into proportion, we're helping to protect ourselves from tormenting anxiety and depression.

Here is the story of Mohammed, who came to England to study mathematics, told in his own words.

CASE HISTORY: MOHAMMED

I was twenty when I left the Red Sea area where my family has lived for generations. My parents saved and saved, and enabled me, their eldest child and only son, to come to England to study. Always I had been bright at mathematics in my country, and when I came abroad I was not fearful – I had had a good grounding and thought I could keep level with my fellow students. But I had not counted on the negative way of thinking my father had inculcated into us, his children, from our earliest age.

Our father was happy that my sisters go to school and that I should be helped most of all, as the possible future provider for my family. But he always kept us very much in check at home – he gave my three sisters impossible tasks to carry out, and would whip me and torment me if I did not work quickly enough on our farm, bring in enough jugs of water from our well or complete my homework from school in time for the prayers he read out every evening. Always he was calling me 'silly boy', 'stupid son', 'spawn of the devil' and other bad names. I felt all right at school because I was good at sport, succeeded in class and had some good friends, some of whose fathers treated them in a similar fashion, but this could not entirely wipe out my father's mockery.

When I came to England, I was determined he and my dear mother would be proud of me. I worked very hard, but the course was not a continuation of what I had learned in my school – it was very different and I kept getting low marks. My father had demanded that I write twice weekly and enclose my up-to-date work report: this was very hard, because although my tutor was encouraging and helpful, saying he thought I would have no trouble keeping up once I had adjusted to the lectures, my father did not see it this way. Getting 50 per cent on a test was an achievement for me, because previous weeks I'd had 20 or 30 per cent. But my father was furious, phoned me at my lodgings, and demanded that I return home (after only two months) and work in his fields. Clearly I was wasting his money . . .

I did not go home – I begged for more time and tried even harder. But every time I came across something I could not make sense of, my mind would start saying to me: 'Useless boy! Upstart! Waste of space and time! You cannot understand because you are stupid. Therefore you are taking your father's hard-earned money deceitfully. You are worth nothing to him and therefore you are not worthy to live. You may as well stop living, and die . . .'

Finally, my father sent me a single air ticket and ordered me to return home within three days. I was so low that I took a lot of paracetamol tablets and some whisky and lay down to die. But my flatmate came back unexpectedly, I was rushed to hospital and my life was saved. When my father was told, he washed his hands of me – he never wanted to hear from me again. The tutors and other university staff were very kind, however. I was sent to see a psychotherapist, who helped me explore the negative trains of thought and depressed feelings that tended to take over when I was under pressure.

When I couldn't do something, I was always calling myself 'stupid boy', 'useless' and 'worthless'. My therapist showed me how to 'contain' the source of the stress by writing it down; then to write next to this what then went through my mind, about myself, my future, other people. I had to jot down my thoughts and beliefs, and the feelings that these led me to have. Then, the challenges – I had to ask myself whether I would believe these things if a friend interpreted his own, similar situation in the same way. What is the evidence against this opinion, and what are the alternatives? Would I think like this if I were not stressed and depressed? And how much belief on a scale of one to a hundred did I have in the alternative explanations?

Finally, I had to write down how much my feelings had changed, on a similar scale of one to a hundred. This and other techniques saved my studies and my life. It works like magic provided you catch your negative thoughts early enough. That's why I bought a very small, hard-covered notebook with a pen attached to it, which is never out of my pocket.

Ruminating

Another form of depressed thinking is called ruminating. Derived from the word 'rumen', meaning a cow's stomach, ruminating is the brain's way of chewing the cud. This could be interpreted as self-indulgent – we're having a good 'wallow' in our misery or worry, and nothing's going to stop us! I think of it more as self-punishment – something many depressed people are startlingly good at. However you view it, letting sad, pessimistic ideas and beliefs take hold, going over and over them in our mind, is a recipe for depression, and for sleepless nights, too, when we toss and turn, plagued by thoughts that refuse to be banished.

Ruminating is different from having automatic thoughts. When we are ruminating, we're not allowing our thoughts and feelings to jump to negative, or other, conclusions. We're consciously allowing a particular train of negative thoughts to take hold, for minutes or hours on end – often repeatedly. We may do it so often that it becomes second nature – spending a day, or even an hour, when those thoughts don't enter our heads, seems inconceivable. And the more we ruminate, the more securely the negative thoughts – and the associated negative feelings – become locked inside our minds.

It's very important to stop this trend, and various methods are available for doing so. If you have only a small rumination problem, stop the thoughts as soon as you become aware of them, and ask yourself something likely to banish them, such as 'Where are these thoughts taking me? Aren't they leading me into depression? Do I really want to go down that route?' If you ruminate so habitually that you're rarely free of the habit try setting a timer on your watch or mobile phone at, say, thirty-minute intervals, and regularly check your thoughts. The most tenacious thinking patterns can be scotched by pattern-interrupt methods, which are outlined in Chapter 7. Meanwhile, here is the story told by Gillian, a fifty-five-year-old women whose daughter was murdered by a paedophile, and whose suffering was increased by her habitual thought patterns centring upon guilt and revenge.

CASE HISTORY: GILLIAN

My little girl Rosemary was five when she was murdered. I was forty-one when I had her – my partner and I had been together for fifteen years and had given up hope of a family, then a miracle happened, and we found I was pregnant. I stopped work six months before our baby was due. We could afford to do without my salary, and we wanted to take every precaution to ensure a safe pregnancy.

Rosemary was born on the expected date, perfect, gorgeous, healthy and the most loved baby on earth. We both idolised her. The three of us couldn't have been happier.

The most terrible day of my life began a week after Rosemary's fifth birthday. Ray and I took her to play on the swings in the park – it was a sunny Saturday in May, and we sat on a nearby bench, keeping an eye on Rosemary. Then an old woman stopped and tried to sell us some white heather. There was no harm in her, she was friendly and made us laugh – and Ray bought a tiny posy for

Rosemary. Then we looked towards the swings, and couldn't see her anywhere. We thought she might be hiding, so we separated, calling and searching everywhere.

After looking for fifteen minutes without success, we both started to panic. I stayed by the swings in case she should return, and Ray went to the police station in the park to report her missing. We could not stop blaming ourselves – and, irrationally, one another – for letting Rosemary out of our sight. We were utterly plagued by guilt. I even began to feel that I was directly responsible for our little girl going missing – as though I were being punished for something (anything) I had done in the past.

Ten days after Rosemary disappeared, we were given the worst news any parent could receive – Rosemary had been found, naked and strangled, in some undergrowth alongside a motorway leading out of London.

They got the man – a known sex offender with a previous conviction for abducting a child, and released from prison on licence due to good behaviour. But his life sentence was no consolation to Ray or to me. I had to go into hospital because I was suicidal – and when I came out after two months, although I was eating and sleeping again, I couldn't get two sequences of thought out of my mind. One was how much I would love to slay Rosemary's killer myself, with my bare hands – I could picture myself doing it with great relish. The other was overwhelming guilt at having allowed my attention to be diverted by the harmless old gypsy woman.

These thoughts were quite normal, in the circumstances. Even I, in my worst moments, could see that. But the thoughts really took over, making it impossible for me do anything that required the least concentration. I gave up trying to read, for a long time – the simplest sentences made no sense to me at all, and my mood was profoundly low. Round and round the thoughts would go.

Eventually I responded sufficiently to my antidepressants to start cognitive behavioural psychotherapy. But it took many months of hard work to banish those hateful, incessant thoughts and to dispense with at least some of the overwhelming burden of guilt.

Gillian's story is tragic, and her reaction to the murder of her little girl is one that most parents could empathise with and understand. Yet clinical depression is not the inevitable outcome of emotional trauma, however monstrous; and Gillian's thoughts and feelings led her firmly in the direction of depression, where she remained until she received anti-depressants and CBT to counteract the destructive thought cycle.

So, when does a rational reaction start to become unhealthy? There is no easy answer to this, but in general we can say that it occurs when a 'normal', that is, usual, expected response to profound loss or trauma fails to resolve over a period of time, and instead becomes deeply entrenched as destructive thought and feeling.

DEPRESSION, SELF-BLAME AND GUILT

As noted earlier (*see page 17*), some experts attribute depression wholly or partly to rage turned inwards, that is, rage directed at the self. This tends to be an analytical argument, and not therefore one you may hear as a depression sufferer seeking cognitive behavioural psychotherapy. But aggression directed at the self is a common, although not invariable, feature of depression, especially in sufferers whose self-esteem is low. There are several ways in which we can attack ourselves when depressed, and we will mention self-blaming first because of the part it played in Gillian's story, told above.

We have all sorts of reasons for blaming ourselves. One of these at least is actually a defensive action against attack on someone or something we love. People who love blindly cannot bear criticism aimed at their partner, child, friend or whomever. Blaming themselves for forgotten birthdays, broken promises and vows or physical violence, which are really down in part or largely to the other person is far less painful than acknowledging faults in the individual they worship. Again, some of us are so used to being blamed for everything that has gone awry since our earliest childhood that blaming ourselves in later life is second nature.

However, although we may feel 'comfortable' (or at any rate, less uncomfortable) accepting the responsibility for accidents and for the behaviour and mishaps of others, it remains a fact that constant self-blame, whatever its source, is a powerful acid, corroding our confidence, self-esteem and sense of self. We tend to blame ourselves more when we're depressed (because this is how depression causes us to think), and the trait of self-blame, conversely, leads us into depression.

Blaming ourselves entirely for things that are not our responsibility, or only partly so, is called personalisation. Gillian did not show this – much of her rage was directed at the perpetrator of the crime – but she still judged herself most harshly. Perhaps you noticed that – apart from a brief interlude at the beginning of this tragedy – there was no blame in her mind directed at her partner who was, after all, as much in charge of their little girl as she was.

Part of Gillian's therapy included writing down alternative views as to where the guilt of that day belonged. For a long time, she could only come up with her name and that of the paedophile. She took several months to acknowledge that Ray's attention, too, had been distracted by the elderly white-heather seller, and that Rosemary herself, although entirely innocent of blame in the adult sense, had played a small role herself in her tragic end. It transpired that she had left the swings and gone down to the pond by herself to see the ducks, something her parents had strictly forbidden her to do.

Self-punishment is another theme associated with self-blaming thoughts and feelings. Depressed people often feel that they are being punished because they are bad; or indeed that they ought to be punished because of the guilt they bear. When this belief is deep-seated and self-forgiveness difficult or impossible, a guilty secret from our childhood can occasionally be responsible. Part of Gillian's task while in therapy was to acknowledge and confront the fact that she had been abused as a small child by an uncle.

This man had not only physically injured and emotionally traumatised the seven-year-old Gillian, but he had also left the usual legacy of guilt connected with paedophilia by telling her that he knew she enjoyed him touching her. He had convinced her that she was therefore 'dirty' and 'bad', which made her readily believe his assertion that a policeman would come and take her away to prison if she, or he, ever disclosed their 'secret'.

In fact, Gillian and Ray's tragedy was followed by happiness. Three years after they lost Rosemary, Gillian conceived again at the age of forty-nine. They were naturally worried about the possibility of having a Down's syndrome child, although it is doubtful whether they would have had a termination in the face of a positive test. As it happened, little Mary Rose was born a healthy and beautiful baby, to the grateful, ecstatic joy of both her parents.

Various physical health boosters promote a balanced mood and aid the action of antidepressants and psychotherapy. We'll see how they can help to relieve depression in the next chapter.

CHAPTER 6

Physical Therapies

We saw in Chapter 2 how 'holism', or the mind, body, spirit approach to healing, recognises the equal importance of our physical, mental and spiritual aspects, all of which need to coexist harmoniously for our health and well-being. Some purists might quibble with the term 'physical therapies' because in treating the body, one is treating the mind and spirit, too. This is, however, a convenient term for therapies applied primarily to the body to optimise health at all levels.

DIET

Leslie and Susannah Kenton's book *Raw Energy*, published in the 1980s, employed naturopathic principles in recommending that we cut down on processed foods and base our meals upon fresh fruits and vegetables, up to 70 per cent of which we should eat raw. It's an incredibly beneficial way of eating for general vigour and mood, if you can get used to it. I recommend that you sensibly limit ready-prepared, sugary and fatty foods, which chemically stress the system, and concentrate on natural foods that boost mood neurotransmitter levels (*see page 39*).

Eating to raise neurotransmitter levels

Tryptophan, an amino acid (protein building block), is the starter substance from which we manufacture serotonin. Five of the foods richest in tryptophan are roast beef, lamb, liver, trout and pumpkin seeds. Chicken breast, shrimps, cod, sesame seeds and roasted peanuts also supply it, as do soya products including soya flour, skimmed milk, cottage cheese and Brazil nuts.

Amino acids (besides other nutrients) have to enter the brain in order to replace worn-out cells and aid in the manufacture of enzymes (chemical helpers), hormones and other cellular substances. However, the brain has a tissue filter called the blood-brain barrier – a sort of anatomical sieve that monitors the molecules entering this organ's substance. Several essential amino acids have to compete at this point for entry into the brain, and the passage across this barrier of tryptophan can be eased by carbohydrates present in the blood from a recent snack or meal. A raised blood glucose level, in fact, gives tryptophan preferential entry into the brain and, by allowing it to 'queue-jump' ahead of other amino acids, promotes serotonin manufacture.

You can therefore maximise the effects on serotonin levels of tryptophan-rich foods by making them the protein part of a main meal (for example, by having a shrimp cocktail, and grilled trout with pumpkin seeds), accompanied by some low-GI foods, such as whole grains and their products. The foods with a low GI, or glycaemic index, release their sugars slowly into the bloodstream, which means that your mood is more likely to be stable and calm than it would be after eating high-GI foods rich in refined sugar. Alternatively, you can save a pudding or dessert (such as yoghurt with high-GI honey, maple syrup or jam, which would raise your blood sugar more rapidly) to snack on two hours later.

Bumping up your blood sugar level like this is perfectly OK if it is done moderately and from time to time – providing you do not suffer from hypoglycaemic symptoms after your blood sugar has returned to normal (these symptoms include feeling jittery, anxious and nervy, a fast pulse, sweating and possibly feeling exhausted and faint as well).

Anecdotal accounts state that babies sleep more soundly if their mother snacks on chocolate while breast-feeding them. The mother's sugar surge resulting from the snack increases the glucose content of her breast milk. The infant's raised blood sugar then enhances the entry of tryptophan from her milk into its brain, where elevated serotonin levels leave it relaxed and drowsy. Many depressed and stressed people who comfort eat describe an almost uncontrollable craving for carbohydrates in all forms. Studies have shown that they respond particularly well to eating more tryptophan-rich foods, and indicate that their craving for carbohydrates may be due partly to low brain serotonin (typical of depression). Tryptophan has also been shown to increase the antidepressant effects of the tricyclic antidepressant drug clomipramine (Anafranil).

For reasons not yet fully understood, depressed people over the age of forty often respond better to an increased intake of phenylalanine. This amino acid ultimately gives rise in the body to adrenaline and noradrenaline; first it is turned into a second amino acid called **tyrosine**, which is then converted into dopa, then dopamine, which gives rise to the two mood neurotransmitters noradrenaline and adrenaline. Phenylalanine is found in the majority of protein food sources, particularly in tryptophan-rich foods, and also in lima beans and chick peas, almonds and walnuts.

Both tryptophan and tyrosine can be taken as dietary supplements, under the guidance of a nutritional expert. However, people with phenylketonuria should stay away from phenylalanine and tyrosine sources (phenylketonuria is a metabolic abnormality present from birth, signs of which are present in the urine of newborn babies, who are routinely tested for it).

Some experts also warn that people being treated with MAOI-antidepressants such as Marplan, Nardil and Marsilid (*see page 68*) should avoid tryptophan and tyrosine taken as nutritional supplements, but this warning has not been issued in connection with these two amino acids' natural food sources. There is also some evidence that small quantities of tyrosine (ie as those present in foods) are *more effective* in increasing brain neurotransmitter levels than larger doses (such as dietary supplements).

Carbohydrates taken within two hours after eating a meal rich in tyrosine similarly enhance its activity. You could combine chick peas or lima beans with toasted almonds, sliced tomatoes, chopped spring onions and a choice of salad leaves, with saffron or herb-flavoured couscous; or make a sandwich of cooked, shredded chicken breast, chopped walnuts and lightly toasted sesame seeds, salad leaves and mayo on whole-grain rye; or snack on Brazil nuts with either dried fruits or a carob or small chocolate bar for a treat.

A slight excess of the trace element **vanadium** may be partly to blame for depression in some people. A number of sufferers in one study were found to improve when they omitted fish and vegetable oil that contained it from their diets for three weeks, and increased their intake of vitamin C, a potent anti-stress factor that also combats this toxicity. Fish and cold-pressed vegetable oils contain important omega fatty acids, however, with many beneficial effects upon the circulation, the brain and other systems, so it is not advisable to eliminate these from your diet for long periods.

A deficiency of **folic acid** has been associated with depression, especially in elderly, confused people and epilepsy sufferers. Elderly, senile people often live in institutions where a diet devoid of fresh foods, a poor appetite, bad or ill-fitting teeth and drug therapy can trigger this vitamin deficiency, which can cause or worsen a tendency to depression, producing a snowball effect. Some anticonvulsant drugs are known to deplete the body of folic acid. Heavy drinkers and people taking aspirin or more than 2g of vitamin C daily may also need extra folic acid.

A serious deficiency may need medical treatment, but you can help to protect yourself by including folic acid-rich foods in your diet. Dark green leafy vegetables such as spinach and broccoli, avocado pears, whole wheat and rye flours, carrots, pumpkins and apricots, liver and egg yolk are all excellent sources.

A shortage of **pyridoxine (vitamin B6)** has been linked to depression in women taking the combined oral contraceptive pill. The oestrogen in the Pill appears to increase the need for this vitamin, which, if not met, can inhibit the manufacture of mood neurotransmitters in the brain. You can guard against this by eating wheat germ and wheat bran, black strap molasses, cantaloupe melon, cabbage, beef, eggs, kidneys and liver, or by taking brewer's yeast as a dietary supplement.

HYDROTHERAPY

The therapeutic use of water dates back to Babylon, ancient Egypt and ancient Greece – in Sparta in ancient Greece, for example, it was decreed that all citizens must take frequent cold baths. Hydrotherapy has been used for many ailments, and is still practised as part of Traditional Chinese Medicine and Native American medicine. Its modern application to depression began with the findings of a nineteenth-century Bavarian, Sebastian Kniepp, who was rejected for the priesthood in 1842 because he had tuberculosis.

Kniepp discovered details of water's therapeutic powers in old Vatican archives, treated and cured himself and, after his eventual ordination, proceeded to apply water remedies to many sick parishioners. In particular, he cured a number of young monks suffering from depression, reportedly by taking them for long, healthy walks in the sunlit mountain air, and insisting that they leap into icy pools whatever the prevailing weather.

Hydrotherapy provides an example of the healthy, stimulating stress we've already looked at (*see pages 44–6*). Its healing abilities stem from the contrasting temperatures and massaging effects it brings, which exploit the body's response to cold and hot stimuli, pressure and the unique sensation of water on the skin. Together, these stimuli activate the nervous and immune systems, and can increase the production and release of stress hormones and mood transmitter chemicals. Cold water contact is used for this purpose in depression because of its stimulating and invigorating action.

Cold showers in themselves could not of course cure depression, but depressed people who take regular cold showers confirm that after such a shower they are aroused from apathy, drowsiness and indifference to their surroundings, and left feeling sharper, brighter and more alert and responsive. Some claim to enjoy a 'brand new, born-again' feeling afterwards, and also to benefit from warm water applications when these are appropriate.

Naturopaths recommending hydrotherapy for depression would suggest that you take warm showers and baths when you're stressed, anxious or suffering from muscular tension. This is common sense, really, and something that we all do daily, or whenever the need arises. You may not have thought of taking two showers (or baths), though, one after the other – a long, relaxed, warm one to relax and soothe you, followed by a short, sharp, cold one to revive you mentally and physically. This combination can be helpful when we're depressed and obliged to cope with the needs of a family, job or whatever, and getting far more tired than normal.

A sauna might cheer you up if you suffer from SAD (*see page 82*), feel the cold in winter and have poor circulation. Whirlpool baths are fun and relaxing, and a cold compress on the forehead eases tension headache. Flotation tanks utilise water or other liquids (and hence are a form of hydro-therapy) to produce a sensation of weightlessness, and are said to be excellent for anxiety and tension, although they do not suit everyone. If you are chronically constipated (a common occurrence in depression) you might like to try one of the oldest forms of hydrotherapy, namely colonic irrigation. Hippocrates is said to have recommended it to help detoxify the system and improve a low mood. Colonic irrigation has many advocates, and is doubtless useful for ridding the bowel of accumulated waste. This in turn purifies the breath, benefits the complexion and reduces body weight by the same weight as the waste matter removed. I have had no personal experience of it, but it is worth trying if you think you might benefit from it.

AROMATHERAPY

Most of us nowadays are familiar with at least some aspects of aromatherapy. Essential oils are sold by nearly all high street pharmacists and health food shops, and a naturopath would probably recommend one or more of these to be used in combination with hydrotherapy. A few drops of pure lavender oil or ylang ylang oil, for example, increase the relaxing effects of a warm bath. Sniffing either essence from the unstoppered bottle or from a drop applied to the inside of the wrist can bring a comforting sense of calmness when your mood is low. You can also pour a few drops on a tissue and tuck it into your bra or top pocket, or under a pillow; rub a little into the inside of your wrist; or add some to a bland carrier oil in an oil burner and allow the heat to dispense the aroma throughout the room. There's more below on the actions of specific essential oils, including lavender and ylang ylang.

The beneficial effects of essential oils are undoubtedly due to the actions of the inhaled compounds on the brain and nervous system, but also, I am sure, to the comforting mental associations many of us make with certain scents. The scent of lavender, for example, may remind us of the security of our childhood home, with its smell of lavender wax furniture polish, while ylang ylang, which smells very much like hyacinths, may awaken the memory of early spring, when hyacinths are in bloom.

Aromatherapy oils can be added to a bland carrier oil for massage and other personal use, but it is extremely important to follow the manufacturer's guidelines and use the essences exactly as advised because they are potent and can be toxic if used in excess. It's equally necessary to ensure that you are using the correct oil if you are treating yourself; commercial considerations aside, many alternative therapists suggest consulting a trained aromatherapist or herbalist who can select the best oil or combination of oils to suit your particular problems at any given time – a person's needs may sometimes change quite rapidly, according to hormonal fluctuations, general health and personal circumstances. Here is some information on several of the most common essential oils used for depression.

Lavender

Lavender essence is prescribed by alternative practitioners to treat depression because it is a great mood balancer. Lavender baths are advised for people who are both depressed and anxious, to help counteract the sleeping problems typical of this disorder. Aromatherapy practitioners generally use massage to apply their oils, and severe mood fluctuations, including those of manic depression, often respond well to lavender oil massaged into the muscles on either side of the spine.

Ylang ylang

This also has specific antidepressant properties, and a calming effect upon nervous system arousal (blood pressure rise,

thumping heart, flushed face) resulting from intense emotion
– especially rage.

Rose

Rose essence is especially useful for depression in women
traumatised by a relationship difficulty or breakdown, especially when the prevailing emotion is grief rather than anger.
It also lifts depression stemming from hormonal changes, being
extensively prescribed to counteract post-natal depression,
menopausal emotional misery and the low mood associated
with premenstrual syndrome.

Essential oil of rose is a renowned and gentle aphrodisiac
(the Romans scattered rose petals on the bridal couch, a custom
reflected in the paper rose petals and other confetti we throw
today). It works well for women who feel ambivalent about
their sexual development, for example some girls and women
with anorexia, and others who doubt their physical attrac-
tiveness (only too common a symptom in depressive illness).
Rose oil is also said to help correct male impotence, and low
libido/lack of sexual arousal in women.

Jasmine

Jasmine oil is traditionally excellent for boosting confidence,
both in yourself and in the future (again, I think that this
probably has something to do with the 'old-fashioned, peaceful' image the essence conjures up).

Neroli

A distillate of the flowers of the bitter or Seville orange tree
named after an Italian princess who used it as her favourite
perfume, neroli is a splendid treatment for acute anxiety.

Clary sage

Clary sage essential oil has been described as a 'euphoric'. It
also has tranquillising properties – it's a potent muscle relaxer,

and is used to treat people suffering from the physical and emotional symptoms of nervous tension and/or those experiencing sleeping problems, symptoms common in depression sufferers.

Clary sage essential oil is distilled from the flowers and flowering tips of *Salvia sclarea*, a plant of singular appearance growing two to three feet high, with spiky flowers and hairy leaves. It is safer to use than common sage oil (from *Salvia officinalis*) because it is less toxic, but it is important to avoid alcohol if you are using it because the combination can cause severe nightmares. (Clary sage oil treatment taken by itself can bring vivid, though not necessarily unpleasant, dreams.)

You can harness the euphoric powers of clary sage by adding a few drops to your bath water and having a long, relaxing bath, or to a massage oil, or by inhaling it from an oil burner. Its reputed aphrodisiac properties are thought to be due in part to its muscle-relaxant activity, since so many sexual problems arise from 'knots of worry' and tension. However, many users report even more positive responses than this explanation suggests, and its ability to trigger colourful dreams points to a more specific action on the brain. It is from this, I believe, that its euphoric powers stem.

Frankincense

Frankincense essential oil comes from resin tapped from the bark of a small tree growing in Middle Eastern countries and North Africa. It has a calming effect on the emotions, and data on its uses suggests that it is especially helpful in getting rid of 'emotional baggage' of the type that tends to dominate our thoughts with traumatic past memories, preventing recovery from depression and optimism about the future.

While not described specifically as a euphoric in the available literature, frankincense does induce the calm, tranquil deep breathing essential to meditation. Anyone with a

Roman Catholic or High Church religious background will be transported by whiffs of frankincense to what some refer to as the 'bells and smells' aspect of worship. The resin is used as incense today and has been for thousands of years; in ancient times it was prized for its ability to drive out demons.

Use frankincense essential oil for massage, inhalations and baths, and as an exotic, beguiling perfume for yourself and for your environment (in oil warmers and burners). For a heady, spiritually uplifting (possibly sublime) experience, use pure frankincense resin, which you can obtain from Church supply shops, and from the sellers of occult and New Age incense/jewellery/books, and so on, which you can easily trace on the Internet and in local newspaper small ads. Buy a proper incense burner to heat the resin – contrived vessels are often unable to cope with the heat and can be dangerous. You will also need the right kind of charcoal to ensure adequate burning; this is available from the same sources.

Bergamot

If you happen to enjoy Earl Grey tea, you will already be familiar with the smoky perfume of bergamot essential oil, which comes from the fruit of a citrus tree first discovered in the countryside around Bergamo in northern Italy, from which it takes its name. Its most important medical use is in the treatment of anxiety and depression. The well-known aromatherapy expert and pioneer Robert Tisserand has called bergamot essential oil 'uplifting'.

In her book, *Aromatherapy: An A–Z*, Patricia Davis refers to bergamot's reputed usefulness in loss of appetite, but says that her own findings suggest, rather, that it acts as an appetite controller, and has proved useful in helping compulsive eaters. She also mentions that the effect is not seen overnight, and requires an empathic working relationship between the therapist and patient.

Use bergamot essential oil as a massage oil (two to three drops added to plain carrier oil), for personal massage; and as bath oil, room fragrance and personal perfume (equally suitable for men and women).

Other essential oils

Besides those described above, aromatic essences that can relieve depression and the symptoms of stress include chamomile, sandalwood, marjoram, black pepper, peppermint, rosemary and thyme.

The massage aspect of professional aromatherapy treatment is particularly beneficial for depression sufferers. When we cannot access – or feel unable to take – closeness and warmth from others, it often 'feels safe' to accept professional physical treatment from a trained expert who, while lacking a personal emotional agenda, nonetheless provides the 'concerned and warm' human contact nearly every depressed person at some level craves. Here is the story told by Beth, aged twenty-two, who took an antidepressant prescribed by her doctor with naturopathic treatment.

CASE HISTORY: BETH

I had always suffered from PMS, with headaches and depression for about ten days each month before my period was due. Then when I was twenty, things started to go wrong – my father died, my mother remarried and I left home and started a relationship that broke up after six months, leaving me emotionally scarred. I had been working as a barmaid, but a management change saw six staff, including me, replaced by newcomers. I was out of work for nine months, and existing on social security.

It got so that I couldn't be bothered to get out of bed in the mornings. I just couldn't face dragging round the shopping centre with no money to buy anything, or sitting about at home, watching daytime TV. In the end, a girlfriend persuaded me to see my GP – the same one who had looked after me as a child. He listened to my symptoms – couldn't keep awake most of the time, pigged out on junk food, no interest in life or in my friends. I told him I just felt so down that I wished I were dead, although I hadn't any plans to kill myself. He told me that I was depressed, and recommended tablets.

I agreed reluctantly, and after a couple of weeks my despair lifted slightly, but the other symptoms stayed the same despite a change of tablets. Then I saw one of the other partners at the practice when my usual doctor was on holiday. He said that he thought I might be helped by naturopathic medicine. I'd never heard of it, but I was prepared to give it a try. The doctor recommended a local practitioner of naturopathy and osteopathy.

I went to see her, and she (Sue) took a full case history of physical and emotional problems. It was easy to talk to her because she was a woman, and I confided in her about my eating. I secretly hated all the chips, chocolate, takeaways and ice cream I was packing away, and hated myself for needing them. My weight was soaring, too, but I couldn't seem to stop. Sue understood – she told me that we often start craving unhealthy foods if we eat too much of them. She explained how natural, low-fat, low-sugar foods with few artificial additives would curb my overeating and help me to lose weight.

I felt much better once I started eating sensibly – I experimented with lots of fresh salads, using made-up salad leaf combinations from supermarkets that I had never tried before, with cottage cheese or prawns. I also ate wholemeal bread, whole grain pasta, brown rice and couscous in place of white bread and chips, and stir-fried chicken or fish instead of battered cod, greasy roasts and white pasta swimming in rich sauces. And I learned how to boost my 'mood chemicals' by eating foods rich in certain amino acids – in place of chocolate and crisps, snacks became pumpkin seeds and Brazil nuts rich in tryptophan, and toasted almonds and walnuts to provide phenylalanine.

The best boost of all, though, came from advice I was sure I would never take. Sue asked me whether I enjoyed showers. I said I did, and she asked me to take a cold one every morning, and another during the day if my mood started to fall, and follow this by massaging in some body lotion she would make up, containing essential oil of rose or geranium to help fight the depression. I thought: 'No way!' I don't even like getting wet in the chilly sea or the rain. But I stayed mildly depressed, sleepy and apathetic – with no enthusiasm for myself or anyone else – and one day I just thought that I might as well give it a go. It was horrid, of course, even though I kept the water tepid and only stayed under the shower for about half a minute. But I told Sue I had tried it and she was delighted. She made me promise to persist, and I asked her to make up two body oils, one of rose and one of geranium, to give me an incentive.

It's surprising what you can get used to! Do you know, I now have a freezing shower every morning on waking, and again during the day if I get drowsy, grumpy or too sorry for myself. Pure rose oil is very expensive, but smells absolutely blissful. I use the rose-scented oil every morning, and the geranium one during the day for any further showers or dips. I am not sure how all this works, but it's certainly doing wonders for me.

MASSAGE

Massage is easier to demonstrate than to describe. It is primarily aimed at relaxing the soft tissues of the body, generally the main muscle groups. While not strictly speaking an holistic therapy in its own right, it is practised by many alternative therapists, including aromatherapists, some osteopaths and chiropractors, naturopaths and sports therapists, and exists in such specialised forms as rolfing, reflexology, applied kinesiology/touch for health and the Feldenkrais technique. I am referring to the straightforward, familiar type of massage here.

When we are depressed, it is possible to become so used to tension, back, neck and shoulder pain, and stress-related headaches that we no longer recognise them for what they are, and attribute the misery they bring to our age, poor general health, the weather and other vexations. Often it isn't until we are finally persuaded to try massage that we realise how much it can improve our energy and well-being.

Like aromatherapy practitioners, masseurs (or masseuses – many are women) either visit clients in their homes, or provide consulting rooms where they can be visited. They generally use a special massage table that provides firm support (beds are too soft) and a hole for the client to breathe through comfortably when lying face downwards. Some may prefer to use a mattress on the floor. The room is always (or ought to be) warm and quiet, and a blanket is provided for the client to retain their modesty when half undressed.

Massage techniques vary according to the desired effect, but when straightforward relaxation is required, the normal practice is to use oil or talcum powder as a lubricant (with an aromatherapy essence added to the oil if applicable), and – at the start – effleurage, which consists of stroking movements to spread the lubricant over the surface of the back.

This may be followed by a number of other techniques, such as friction, energetic rubbing and petrissage, a kneading process that works upon the underlying soft tissues and fatty layer, stretching shortened muscles and tissues, loosening knots in contracted muscles and easing areas of fibrositis (small protrusions of muscular tissue through a muscle's outer sheath, aggravated by nervous tension and causing an acute, stabbing sort of pain between the shoulder blades). Other techniques include clapping the skin over an area with cupped hands, pummelling and a motion of the fingers like piano playing, often used for painful areas at the base of the neck.

The immediate effect of massage can be stimulating or relaxing, according to your needs. It is not intended to be painful in the negative sense, but it can produce a unique sort of pleasurable pain that you have to experience to understand. Tender areas are bound to be located if you suffer from tension and stiff muscles, and the most satisfactory approach is to locate, or have recommended to you, a qualified and experienced masseur, answer all the questions relevant to your difficulties when they take a case history, then relax and leave it to them. It is also advisable, if you decide to try massage, to go ahead with it sooner rather than later. The longer problems persist (including mood and stress-related ones), the longer and harder it usually is to gain full relief.

HERBAL REMEDIES

Holistic medical herbalists view depression as arising for a number of reasons, and generally requiring treatment by a qualified practitioner over weeks or months. This similarity with the conventional view ends here, however, for herbalists are generally opposed to antidepressant drugs, and aim their remedies at correcting imbalance between the mind, body and emotions/spirit. For mild to moderate depression, my experience is that herbal medicine has a lot to offer, but I remain convinced that a course of antidepressants is essential for severe or recurrent illness.

St John's wort (hypericum)

This has been available in the UK as an over-the-counter herbal remedy for all but severe depression since the 1990s, although it has been used in Germany and elsewhere in Europe for far longer. You can buy the tablets at most high street pharmacies and health food shops, and the recommended dose of its active ingredient, hypericum, is 30mg three times daily. They are a good antidote to the stressed out feeling many depression sufferers experience and, like prescribed antidepressants, take two to three weeks to produce their optimum effect.

Like other herbal remedies, you should avoid St John's wort when pregnant or breast-feeding, and also when taking a pharmaceutical antidepressant. St John's wort has also been found to interfere with the effectiveness of an AIDS remedy (indinavit), the anti-tissue rejection drug cyclosporine prescribed for heart transplant patients, the anticoagulant warfarin, and oral contraceptives. If you are taking prescribed medicines of any kind, check with the herbal remedy's manufacturers or your GP for any incompatibility. You certainly will not need both the herbal remedy *and* antidepressant drugs, and I do urge you not to replace the latter (and/or tranquillisers such as Ativan or Valium) with St John's wort or any other natural remedy without consulting your doctor.

You should combine a course of St John's wort with other complementary treatments, such as a healthier diet, exercise, aromatherapy oils and meditation as recommended in this book.

Other useful herbal remedies

Other herbal preparations with a good reputation as depression treatments include oats (which you can simply include in your diet), damiana, vervain, Asiatic ginseng, rosemary, skullcap, lady's slipper and lavender (remember its usefulness as an aromatherapy treatment?). All these have different applications and, for a condition such as depression, should be prescribed by a qualified herbal therapist after a full consultation and health discussion.

EXERCISE THERAPY

While regular exercise is of great benefit to many depression sufferers, it is probably the last thing you feel like doing. Sebastian Kniepp's depressed monks were surely most unenthusiastic, too, about the vigorous, challenging walks he took them on when they were feeling low. However, the aerobic activity this involved must have played a part in their recovery, alongside the benefits of skinny dipping in freezing cold mountain streams. This type of exertion, and the less challenging stretch-and-bend sort of exercise, are both useful in combating depression and symptoms of stress.

Many research trials into exercise's benefits have supported this claim. One of them, known as the SMILE study (standing for Standard Medical Intervention and Long-term Exercise), compared the effects of exercise and antidepressant drugs on depression. Reported in the *Journal of Ageing and Physical Activity*, it involved 156 people aged between fifty and seventy-seven with a major depressive disorder. Patients with the milder symptoms showed most improvement, both in their low mood and their mental function. Attention, concentration and the ability to perform manual tasks requiring mental output remained the same, but patients improved in many other respects.

Regular exercise was found to improve the ability to reason and think logically. It also enhanced short-term memory (the sort most affected by Alzheimer's disease and other kinds of dementia), and the ability to plan and organise, and to do several different things at the same time. Factors responsible for the improved mental function are believed to include more efficient blood circulation to the brain, keeping it better supplied with oxygen and vital nutrients; less tension and better ability to handle stressful events; better sleep and appetite; and the ability to think more clearly due to improved mood resulting from better mood neurotransmitter production.

Physical benefits due to regular exercise which reduce the symptoms of depression include easier weight control (and loss of surplus fat, leading to improved self-esteem and confidence); higher levels of energy and physical stamina; stronger muscles, reducing the fatigue and exhaustion aspects of depression; fewer headaches, muscular aches and pains, and migraine attacks; and anti-ageing effects (also self-esteem boosters!).

Some experts believe that the rejuvenating effects of regular aerobic activity (besides the improvements already listed) may be due to increased release of growth hormone from the brain's pituitary gland. Supplements of human growth hormone (HGH) have been used to promote youthfulness, maintain lean body mass rather than surplus fat (which in turn utilises the calories in food fuel more effectively), and improve vitality, the overall appearance of youthfulness and active brain power. What is certain is that regular exercise causes improved circulation to all areas, including the skin of the face and neck, and helps to deter wrinkles and lines, and improves the complexion. The enjoyment of love-making also gets better as we become more flexible (physically and mentally), with improved self-esteem and more energy. Additionally, depression-linked constipation tends to disappear with regular exercise, and the digestion and enjoyment of food improves.

AEROBIC EXERCISE

Useful, healthy aerobic exercise does not mean jogging, cycling up steep hills or having to join (and use!) a gym. It is the kind of exercise that makes each of us, as individuals, perspire slightly and become a bit out of breath – though not sufficiently for conversation to become laboured. We have all heard of the 'high' experienced by long-distance runners and other athletes who push themselves to the limits. *Your* limit may be walking briskly for twenty minutes, or swimming three or four lengths of a swimming pool – it all depends on your state of fitness to begin with.

What you choose to do depends upon your circumstances and the time you have available – just make sure that it depends equally upon your inclinations and taste. If you loathe swimming, there is no point in trying to take it up. If, on the other hand, you have a bicycle you haven't used for ages, but think you might like to, get it out on a sunny day and limit yourself to, say, ten minutes at your first attempt. Build up slowly to longer intervals of exercise as your confidence starts to return and your depression starts to lift.

Exercise, in the main, is self-treatment; but it is precisely what a psychotherapist or your doctor would recommend for depression if you discussed it with them. If you haven't the oomph! to get started because of your depression, either ask a friend to join you or consider joining a pleasant, not-too-demanding class of something like aquaerobics or gentle keep fit. To be of best use to the body's metabolism (and to raise a low and depressed mood), you need to exert yourself aerobically for twenty to thirty minutes four to five times a week. And if none of this appeals to you (but you crave the improved energy and emotional lift all the same) – then opt for the simplest exercise in the world.

Change into comfortable walking shoes, walk out of your front door and head off briskly in any direction you fancy for five minutes – timed by your watch. Then turn around and return home. You have now completed your first 'aerobic exercise session' and should congratulate yourself on your achievement. Keep on receiving the antidepressant benefits of exercise by giving yourself small goals, feeling comfortable with one achievement (say, three twenty-minute walks a week) before tackling another. Never berate yourself if you miss a planned session – and if you have any health problems for which you receive regular treatment, do consult your doctor before taking up regular exercise.

Stretch exercises

Stretch exercise routines, such as yoga and pilates, benefit the mind and emotions as well as making the body more supple (*see also* Chapter 8). However, it is important not to make too many changes at once. It is easy to build simple stretches into the structure of your day, to ease clenched muscles, help you relax and bring calmness and tranquillity when stressed.

You can start by wriggling and stretching before getting out of bed in the morning. Stretch your arm, leg, stomach, buttock and back muscles gently, then have a warm shower, followed by a short, sharp, cold one (or better still, just the cold one).

Take regular breaks during the day, especially if you spend hours driving or sitting at a desk, and do some stretching during your breaks. Movement – as well as fresh air – can help to dispel the sort of uncontrollable stress that builds up when we confine ourselves (often unwillingly) to the same space for hours on end. Taking time out by walking away from a challenging scene, preferably into the fresh air and out of the range of irritating voices or music, can help to maintain sanity and temper, and quell an incipient low mood.

HOMOEOPATHY

Like some other natural treatments, homoeopathic remedies can be either self-administered or prescribed by a family GP or by a qualified (homoeopathic) practitioner. This form of treatment has the potential to help a majority of conditions, especially long-term, chronic ones, such as depression and anxiety disorders. It's a simple matter of selecting an appropriate remedy (which is the name for all homoeopathic medicines) from a pharmacist or health food store, to relieve toothache, for instance, or to treat minor cuts and bruises. For a condition such as depression, however, where suiting the remedy to the patient is essential to the success of the treatment, I would recommend consulting an expert.

A lot of nonsense is spoken about homoeopathy, not least by medical doctors, always excepting those who take the trouble to study and prescribe homoeopathic remedies because they are safe and they work. The main point of contention is the fact that the remedies contain extremely small quantities of active substance – in fact, the more they are diluted, the more potent they become. The most common joke at homoeopathy's expense is that if its principle were true, one could get merrier on half a thimbleful of whisky than on half a dozen doubles. But homoeopathy doesn't work like that.

Homoeopathy began when its founder Dr Samuel Hahnemann, a young doctor born in Saxony over 200 years ago, started to look around for gentler forms of medical treatment in the first part of the nineteenth century. Appalled by such barbaric practices as bleeding patients nearly to death, boring holes in their skulls and giving them emetics to make them violently sick, he started to review the effects of some commonly prescribed drugs. Using himself as a guinea pig he discovered, first of all, that quinine, prescribed for malaria, produced malaria-type symptoms of fever and profuse sweating in someone in good health. He assumed that the symptoms that occur in real malaria were not due to the blood parasite that causes it, but were signs of the body trying to fight it off.

Hahnemann found the same with the other medicines he tried: the drug that produced certain symptoms in a well person was the drug of choice to treat those symptoms when someone became ill with them. This led him to draw up the fundamental tenet of homoeopathy – that 'like cures like'. A similar discovery was made and taken a step further by Dr Edward Jenner in Britain. Acting on the hearsay that a mild attack of cowpox prevented infection in the future with the deadlier smallpox, Jenner inoculated patients with vaccine made from cowpox pus. He found that this did, indeed, confer immunity.

Hahnemann then discovered that the potency of a remedy was not related to its strength (that is, its concentration in solution) but to how many times it had been diluted. If a substance were diluted a hundred times in distilled water, for instance, the resultant drug 'proving', as he called it, was more and not less effective.

Homoeopathic treatment has developed a great deal since its founder's day, and a wide spectrum of plant, mineral and animal derivatives are used to make up the remedies. Most (although not all) are in tablet form, and powerful ones, such as ARS or arsenic chloride at 60x potency, are believed not to contain more than an atom or two of the active ingredient. Research and controversy have stemmed from this anomaly, and one explanation is that the prolonged and repetitive shaking of an active ingredient in its carrier substance imprints the unique vibratory pattern of that constituent's molecules with increasing definition, as dilution succeeds dilution.

This seems far-fetched to many people, but less so perhaps to many quantum physicists, who now believe that all material objects, however materially dense, consist of electromagnetic energy at various vibratory wave lengths. If mass is no more than energy in motion, there is every reason for believing the explanation put forward to explain how homoeopathic remedies work. For they certainly do work for many people. This is why they are available on NHS prescription, why homoeopathy is recognised by an act of Parliament, and why the waiting lists at London's Royal Homoeopathic Hospital are as long as, if not longer than, those at orthodox hospitals. It also doubtless explains why Her Majesty Queen Elizabeth is reputed to take a selection of homoeopathic remedies with her wherever she travels.

The remedies

Arsenic chloride is prescribed in various potencies to relieve depression and feelings of despair. BAPT – extract of *Baptisia tinctoria* (wild indigo) – suits certain types of depression, as do CALC (Calcarea – oyster shell), GELS (gelsemium or yellow jasmine – remember the importance of jasmine essential oil as an aromatherapy depression treatment?), SEP (Sepia – cuttle fish), VALE (valerian) and LIL – T (*Lilium tigrinum* or tiger lily). HYPER (Hypericum – St John's wort) is recommended for depression following an operation, an accident or a fright (and is a herbal remedy, too, used in ordinary quantities), while SEP (*Sepia officinalis* – cuttlefish) and PHOS (phosphorus) relieve depression in the days leading up to a period.

If you look through a book of homoeopathic remedies, besides the names of the active compounds and the complaints which they relieve, you will see mention of personal characteristics such as 'pale-faced with freckles', 'timid with fair hair', 'feels worse when it rains' and '(his/her symptoms) aggravated by a cold north wind'. This is because the individuality of each one of us (as recognised by the holistic theory) is centrally important in homoeopathic practice, and the skill and experience of a practitioner is directed towards identifying precisely the right remedy for a person, taking into consideration temperament, past medical history, physical appearance, emotional problems past and present, and external irritants that aggravate their problem. To get the best out of homoeopathic remedies – especially in the case of young babies, elderly people and those who are frail in other ways – it really is essential to consult a homoeopathic practitioner.

There is a striking parallel between this thinking and the highly individualised personal stress factors that cause so much personal trauma, which we looked at in Chapter 3. Here is the story told by Myrtle, aged ninety, whom I treated for depression and stress.

CASE HISTORY: MYRTLE

I first went into residential care six years ago, after my husband Len died and my arthritis made it too hard to cope alone. I liked the home – I knew several ladies there in my age group, and the staff were lovely to us. We each had our own room, unless we asked to share. My friend Madge joined the care home eighteen months ago, when I had been there for nearly five years. We were on the point of asking to share a double suite when the terrible news came that the home was going to close.

Everyone was so upset. The doctors of the various residents got up a petition requesting that the council come up with the extra £11.50 a week per resident needed to keep the home open, but they wouldn't. They had already spent the year's funds on a sort of community centre in a nearby town – I won't say what sort. It made me very angry and my feelings about it are not politically correct.

Madge and I were parted, and she died three weeks later. I had been shunted into a cold, draughty old home, where the staff were not interested in the residents, and we had to share, two or three to a room, whether we wanted to or not. I couldn't eat or sleep, cried all day and refused to take my tablets. What was the point? They'd only keep me alive and I very much wanted to die and be with Len and Madge once more.

Then the doctor visited and diagnosed depression. She made me see that, sad as the recent events had been, depressive illness was making things worse, and far harder for me to cope. She offered me an antidepressant, and I agreed I would take one if necessary (I knew in my heart that this is what Len would have wanted me to do) – but I asked her whether I could try a homoeopathic remedy first. I had been reading about homoeopathy in a women's magazine, and it said that the remedies, which were effective in many sorts of conditions, were entirely safe and free of side effects, and suitable for everyone – newborn infants, elderly, frail people like myself, and others on ordinary prescription medicines.

The doctor was delighted I'd suggested this, and prescribed BAPT and GELS [see above] to take on alternate days, in potencies of 60x and then 6x. I didn't feel any different at first, but after a couple of months – and a three-week holiday with my granddaughter and her family during which I was made a lot of fuss of – I started to improve greatly. My granddaughter also bought me a little oil warmer for essential oils, and three essences to try. I went on using the homoeopathic remedies for a year, and still use CALC regularly. I enjoy using the oil several nights a week, too, and during the day if I spend an hour alone (we now all have a room of our own). I use my original three – jasmine, rose and lavender – but I think the lavender one suits me best.

BACH FLOWER REMEDIES

This treatment system originated with Dr Edward Bach (pronounced *batch*), a conventional physician born in Britain towards the end of the nineteenth century. He held posts at University College, London, and at the London School of Immunology, before becoming a pathologist and bacteriologist at the London Homoeopathic Hospital in March 1919. The homeopathic principle of treating the patient rather than the disease with natural remedies (*see* homoeopathy, *pages 125–8*) impressed Edward Bach profoundly, and he took to studying patients' personalities rather than their physical symptoms. He concluded that disease arises from problems of the mind and emotions, and directed his therapy at their inner conflicts through the use of plants, of whose properties he had a unique and intuitive knowledge.

His techniques rely on capturing the essential energy concentrated within flowers, just as drops of dew or rain absorb the properties of the petals to which they cling under the influence of sunlight. Dr Bach prepared his remedies similarly, acting upon the age-old belief in the four elements of air, earth, fire and water. Freshly picked flowers were placed on the surface of a glass bowl of (natural) water, and left to stand in the sun for three hours. The vibrational energy released into the water from the flowers by the sun then provided the 'stock' from which the diluted products – the remedies – were made up. An equal volume of brandy was added as a preservative, before the remedies were bottled.

Dr Bach spoke of the plants' power to 'elevate our vibration' and draw down spiritual power, cleansing mind and body and providing relief. Many of us accept that herbs heal by an interaction between their energy fields and ours (*see* homoeopathy's mode of action, *page 126*), and Dr Bach's remedies can be seen as an extension of this. Some complementary practitioners suggest or prescribe these remedies, but much of the treatment is in the form of self-help. Leaflets are often available on the remedies wherever they are sold (in pharmacies and health stores), and there are a number of detailed books on the topic (*see* Further Reading, *page 177*).

Most of the remedies are taken as a drop or two on the tongue, but they are also made up as greaseless ointments with a homoeopathic base. The usual dose by mouth is three to five drops two to three times a day in fresh, pure mineral water or freshly squeezed fruit juice, or placed directly on the tongue. They are entirely non-toxic (although you should check that you have no allergies to a particular plant remedy you are considering taking), and are equally suitable for elderly, frail people, newborn babies, animals and even plants. Here are three remedies that might suit you if you are depressed.

Agrimony
This is typically useful if you appear carefree, yet inwardly feel tortured and tormented, if you hate being alone, have a tendency to misuse drugs or alcohol under stress, and have churning, wretched thoughts (you may also have the positive qualities of making light of pain and illness, prove a good companion who can laugh at your own worries and be distressed by quarrels and arguments).

Clematis
This remedy could be right for you if you are listless, indifferent and lacking energy, have poor concentration, prefer your own company and tend to sleep very heavily (positive qualities might be sensitivity to inspiration, being realistic and purposeful at times, and being an idealist with creative bents in healing, art or drama).

Honeysuckle

This could suit you if you are depressed with homesickness and/or nostalgia, suffer from regrets and live in the past, tend to lose interest in the present and fear what lies ahead (your positive qualities might include the ability to view experience as valuable, and to lay it to rest and progress confidently from it into the future).

In the next chapter, we'll look at other, personalised self-help methods directed at combating depression for each of us as individuals.

CHAPTER 7

Self-help Methods

In my first book on depression, published in 1984, I described several self-help methods for dealing with negative emotions, which the *Nursing Times,* in a favourable review, referred to as 'homespun'. I *did* spin them on the home hearth – from ideas based on my own experience and reading, from visualisation methods suggested by my ex-husband David Shreeve, a hypnotherapist, and from hints and tips gathered over the years from friends, colleagues and patients.

Many readers wrote to tell me how much the book had helped them. I have updated some of the self-help advice in the light of research developments, but it's essentially as simple and straightforward now as it was then. It would not be of much use to me or to other depression sufferers if it were otherwise.

Can we help ourselves when we're depressed? Yes, we can, provided we've *some* energy and motivation to put to work on our behalf. The techniques described here are not intended as a substitute for the normal grieving process that (perhaps with skilled help) runs its course and is ultimately resolved. But they can be used by themselves for mild to moderate depression, or to supplement psychotherapy exercises between treatment sessions, if the therapist is agreeable. They don't come easily to everyone – you need to be able to visualise objects and situations and to practise the techniques at least daily to obtain their full benefit.

If your motivation and energy levels are low, it can be very useful to have someone share the exercises with you, especially in the early stages, just to get you going (they are useful for non-depressed people, too). If you're really too low for self-help techniques, see your doctor if you haven't already done so, and try them once your antidepressant has kicked in and you're starting to feel better.

ATTITUDE – ATTITUDE – ATTITUDE

We've already seen that small shifts in thinking can produce big improvements in mood. Attitude isn't easy to define, although we all know what it means. More entrenched than 'opinion', it's the product of our personality traits, prejudices, thoughts and ideas, it's heavily invested in emotion, and it influences our mood and our reactions to situations and to people. Some negative attitudes have their uses – 'I'd surely die if I experimented with recreational drugs', for example, or 'I am not strong emotionally – I'd never survive a destructive relationship'. But a negative or obstructive attitude to life and people in general impairs how we function on many levels, and can lead to and intensify depression.

Starting with our attitude to depression itself, feeling negative and hopeless about it makes it harder to cope, and also hinders recovery. It's been known for a long time that believing that we will get over cancer (and other serious illnesses) gives us a better chance of doing so. A February 2004 study reported in *Cancer* journal and the national press suggested that people who kept cheerful when diagnosed with serious illness fared no better than those with negative outlooks. But these findings have been strongly contested by data gathered over decades from research and from anecdotal evidence. As discussed earlier, belief and hope in our self-healing powers boost the immune system and help the body fight back. Whatever benefits our physical selves inevitably benefits our mind and emotions, too.

EASING DEPRESSION'S GRIP

How do you picture your depression? What do you see in your mind when your mood is low? Is there a ball of lead inside your chest, a dark cloud engulfing you, an endless, dreary tunnel in which you are wandering, lost? One way to overcome your vulnerability to depression – that sinking acceptance that the condition is impossible to fight, and will always blight your life – is radically to change this image. Cut the enemy down to size!

St Anthony's depression was 'the devil that stalks by noonday'. Winston Churchill's was his 'black dog' – powerful metaphors for a fearful enemy. Call yours something daft, a name that brings a smile (however briefly) to your face – Fido or Bonzo, Thunderbum or Uglychops (or something much ruder), it truly doesn't matter. Mock it! Set up a laugh at its expense! You don't have to tell anyone about this unless you feel like it; just make sure that you substitute this name whenever 'depression' enters your head.

Now instead of saying, 'I am depressed' – which cedes victory to the enemy even before he's finished pitching his tents on the battlefield – think of yourself as *having* Fido/Bonzo. 'Having' rather than 'being' implies some distance between yourself and it. Your 'I' – your essential self – which remains whole and entire, is temporarily saddled with an ailment. Yes, an *ailment!* Named Fido/Bonzo. A head cold is an ailment – you can feel really ill with one, if you're unlucky – but it doesn't pervade your whole being, it's not life threatening and you know that, despite it, you remain essentially healthy. A head cold is *a nuisance* – not a national crisis. Try to think of your depression in similar terms.

Now you can replace doom and gloom about your low mood with this approach: 'Oh dear, Fido's at the door . . . !' or 'That wretched Uglychops has come back!' And you can visualise Fido or Uglychops not as a black cloud, a tunnel or a many-tentacled monster squeezing you to death, but as a troublesome imp, a mischievous gremlin, perhaps a Gollum-like character from *The Lord of the Rings*, who would cause you grief if you let it. Sure, it needs dealing with, and we all know what a nightmare depression can be. But you are already starting to question Fido/Bonzo/Uglychops's ability to harm you; you're starting to see that succumbing (further) to a low mood is not inevitable and you're wresting the power away from this condition and into your own hands – where it belongs.

You can distance yourself further by placing Fido/Bonzo (who's much smaller and weaker than you) somewhere where you can keep an eye on him – cavorting around your ankles, perhaps, or trying to peep over your shoulder. Did you ever hear of the 'naughty monkey'? If I were naughty as a small child, my mother would often say that a 'naughty monkey on my shoulder' had made me cheeky, disobedient or whatever. She'd pretend to knock it away, and I would join in. Sometimes we'd chase him down the lavatory and pull the plug – or out of the front door, which I then slammed, very hard – or into the fire, where we'd watch him go up the chimney in smoke.

Of course, she and I knew that no monkey like those in the zoo was really around tempting me – we weren't daft and neither are you, and you will be equally clear that Fido/Bonzo exists solely within your imagination. But the imagination is immensely powerful. It can be used to counter, instead of to enhance, depression, and picturing depression in this way is a step towards easing its grip. It's worth noting that this 'distancing' technique does not deny your depression's existence, or its potential to harm you. What it does is to acknowledge it as an undesirable alien that you can control and neutralise, if you wish.

DESPATCHING YOUR DEPRESSION

You've reduced the enemy's importance, so what are you going to do with an ugly little imp with a belittling nickname, now that it's around your ankles waiting to trip you up, or on your shoulder about to whisper miserable thoughts into your ear? Get rid of it like I did the monkey! Knock it off and jump on it! Kick it in the backside and watch it zoom over your head and up into the sky, where the sunlight shrivels it up, or the winds buffet it to smithereens or the clouds absorb it and wash it away in cleansing rain. We'll be looking at safe, simple ways of doing this in a moment. Here is the story related by John, aged fifty-four, who had been depressed since being made redundant four years previously.

CASE HISTORY: JOHN

I was a senior hair stylist working for a large shipping company with cruisers and trading vessels travelling throughout Europe, North Africa and the Far East from several British ports. I loved the job and the way of life – I'd been with them since my late twenties, and was as well paid as you get in that line of hairdressing. I was always on certain cruises – Gran Canaria over Christmas and January; Spain, Portugal and northern Italy in the spring; Hong Kong island and parts of China in the early summer; and Greece in the late summer and early autumn.

Of course, I built up my own clientele – officially, stylists didn't have their 'own' customer lists, but lots of people go on the same cruise year after year, and they get to know the staff – as we got to know them. I could always be sure of at least a dozen familiar faces on the big summer trips, and one regular client told me that she had asked when I would be working so that she could plan her holiday to fit in. Booking staff weren't supposed to give out this information, but concessions were made for the 'regulars'.

We did hear, a few months before any redundancies were

announced, that one or two cruises were being withdrawn, but there was no hint of real concern. Then one day, just after I stepped ashore from an archaeology trip around the Greek mainland – the sort where there's a specialist lecturer to talk about the antiquities and ancient sites – I was asked to attend a meeting at head office. The human resources boss did not beat about the bush (he'd only been in the job five minutes, and looked young enough to be my grandson), and told me bluntly that they were getting rid of me.

I felt winded – gutted. I couldn't eat or sleep (I don't drink, or I might have taken to the bottle), and I cried a lot at home with just my cat for company. Finally a neighbour called by and hardly recognised me. She asked the doctor to call. He diagnosed depression and prescribed tablets. I refused to go into hospital, but agreed to see a psychotherapist.

I didn't think psychotherapy could help, and I was too low to care. But I saw the therapist twice a week, and when I started to feel better, she got me to select a name for my low mood – I called it Big Roy after a bully I hated at school – and asked me to picture it as a nasty hobgoblin or something. Because I'm a *Lord of the Rings* fan I chose an orc – a small one. Surprisingly, none of it felt daft – she explained that treatment for depression did not have to be difficult or nasty, and that to believe otherwise was partly down to the depression.

I did what she asked – being redundant, I had plenty of time to practise – and I got a real kick myself out of booting Big Roy the orc in the backside (I used an old football), and imagining him frying in the sun. She taught me other tricks (she called them exercises) and, together with the antidepressant, my depression had cleared up within six months.

SPECIFIC NEGATIVE EMOTIONS

The technique described above can be adapted to deal with a generalised negative attitude. Perhaps you are already seeing a therapist, or working on your depression by yourself, to identify responsible thoughts. You discover that your auto-matic thoughts frequently cascade down to fundamental beliefs such as, 'I am a loser', 'I am a waste of space/ugly/unattractive' or something similar. You also find, from writing down your thoughts, that you often 'ruminate' (*see page 99*), going over and over grievances or tragedies from your present or past, and/or bleak foreshadows of your future. It becomes clear that your disenchantment with life and other people stems from, and flourishes upon, bitterness, grief, jealousy, remorse, resentment and/or other negative emotions. Your attitude is causing major problems in your relationships at work and at home, and obstructing your happiness and self-development. Having recognised the problem, you can start the attitude-busting exercise.

Start by writing a list of *all* your negative ideas, thoughts and feelings – including any you are ashamed of. We all have thoughts and feelings we'd rather not own – it's an inescapable part of being human. Take your time, think hard, and capture every one of them. Now ask yourself: 'If my best mate/girlfriend/lover had these thoughts/feelings and was unhappy/depressed/couldn't get on with life (just like me), what would I advise them to do?' You will soon realise that these thoughts and feelings are carrying you deeper and deeper into depress-ion and 'learned helplessness'. Ask yourself whether you want, whether you ought or can afford, to take this route.

Assuming that your answer is 'no', you need to let go of these emotions, one at a time. Single out whichever one is causing you the most grief. Be ruthless. You may find this hard, and will perhaps learn that success doesn't happen overnight – entrenched feelings become part of our psyche's fabric. They can become safe and familiar to us, and we can fear that gaining freedom from them will cause a rent that can never be repaired. It may help you to compare getting rid of bad feelings with lancing a painful abscess and draining out infect-ious pus.

Another reason why destructive feelings and worry or rumination patterns can be difficult to get rid of is that to us, they are usually *justified*. Perhaps your partner has left you through no fault of your own. Or you've been passed over for promotion because a new boss has allocated the post elsewhere. Or, after working and saving for years, you find that there's insufficient endowment money to pay off your mortgage, or that your smaller than expected pension means that you must postpone your planned retirement.

Alternatively (or also), you may have lost a loved one, had your home ransacked, been mugged and robbed, are going deaf, never hear from your children/parents, can't cope much longer without a home help. You were probably not responsible for any of these traumas, but even if you were, it doesn't alter the facts or how you've responded emotionally to them. Indeed, what you are feeling is what anyone would feel in the same situation.

The important question is: do you *really* want to penalise yourself further by becoming/remaining depressed? This sounds as though I am suggesting that your depression (your Fido/Bonzo) is your fault. I'm not, and it isn't. You have suffered one or more personal catastrophes, from which negative automatic thoughts have taken root. You are unhappy or bitter, angry or sad, about your life and some of the people in (or not in) it. *But you cannot punish anyone else, or alter circumstances, by punishing yourself.* Your negative attitude (this term is sometimes used pejoratively, but that is certainly not how I am using it here) and the thoughts you mull over constantly in your mind are causing you unnecessary suffering. It's time to replace this attitude with self-nurturing thoughts and feelings leading towards personal fulfilment.

Looking at your list, you have decided which emotion to tackle first. Sit down with a large sheet of plain paper in front of you, and draw a balloon – large, round or oblong, with the mouthpiece towards you, tied with a little string. In the balloon's centre, write the name of the emotion you want to tackle first – bitterness, anger, jealousy or whatever, and draw a ring around it. Then draw a number of smaller circles around the central one, and within each of these, write a word or two – for example, the event that gave rise to it (such as bereavement, divorce or loss of job), the name or names of any people who helped to cause it (give each their own circle), a negative thought or two that arises from it – just sufficient, in fact, for you to identify them at a glance. Then draw a line from each small circle leading to the larger one, producing a diagram like the one below.

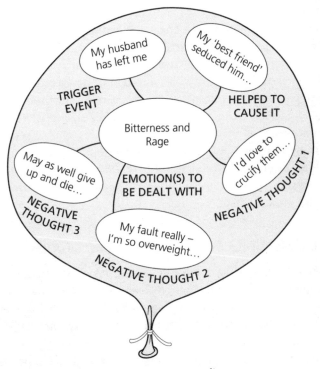

An example of an emotions diagram

Take a good, long look at the diagram – it won't be around for much longer. Fold it carefully, and keep it with you in a handbag or pocket. Look at it briefly once or twice during the day, and keep it somewhere within reach overnight. Then spend half an hour the next day on one of the relaxation methods described in this book (*see Chapter 8*) and, when you are tranquil physically and mentally, take a final look at your emotions diagram. Close your eyes and see the balloon, now filled with helium, floating above your head at the end of its string. See yourself taking it to the window, releasing it and watching it float right up into the sky. You can either imagine it floating out of sight and being absorbed harmlessly into the atmosphere, or dart an Exocet mental missile at it, blowing it to smithereens. Later you will learn how you can do this most effectively with a the help of affirmations (*see page 148*). Finally, tear your emotions diagram into tiny pieces and burn them, or bury them in the garden.

Once you have dealt with your central problem, you can turn your attention to any further negative emotions you need to lose. This technique is also useful for losing unwanted habits such as drinking too much alcohol, smoking, over-eating and using addictive substances; but it's advisable to obtain additional help from your GP, Alcoholics Anonymous, Narcotics Anonymous or a similar support organisation if you have an addiction problem.

BANISHING NEGATIVE EMOTIONS

The techniques I have talked about so far can be immensely helpful in dealing with a range of negative emotions. Ridicule your enemy depression, cut him down to size, challenge his ability to harm you, arm yourself with positive thoughts that can drive him away for good. However, some negative feelings require more than this to loosen their hold on our psyche. Shame and guilt are examples.

Shame

This is a highly destructive emotion plaguing many depressed people. Depression typically distorts our perception of our qualities, abilities and value to others, and these negative thoughts need to be dealt with if we are to recover. However, a conviction that we're inherently inferior that persists even when we're not depressed can so paralyse our will to get better that helping or receiving help with our depression becomes more problematic.

According to Paul Gilbert, Professor of Clinical Psychology at the University of Derby, we all have the capacity to feel shame, although this is hard to believe of certain individuals, particularly psychopaths who neither learn from their mistakes nor experience remorse. Professor Gilbert makes some interesting points on shame's origins, however. In his book *Overcoming Depression* (*see* Further Reading, *page 177*) he explains it as an alerting mechanism that has evolved as a component of the human mind to warn us of potentially dangerous situations, such as 'being rendered inferior or subordinate, rejected or ostracised'. We can then avert attack by behaving submissively, avoiding eye contact, for instance, or using other subordinate body language.

Experiences in infancy and early childhood can also generate shame, particularly repeated experiences of being made to feel that we are never good enough (or in the way, unwanted or whatever); the pressure to conform to standards that don't suit us as individuals; and the experience of being verbally and physically attacked.

Some of the most common negative thoughts involve shame – for example, 'I am unattractive/a loser/no good at x or y.' These often come from what cognitive therapists call all-or-nothing thinking and over-generalisations. Perfectionists tend to be all-or-nothing thinkers, imagining that they must achieve everything perfectly, in record time, to be any good. And all depressed people have a tendency to over-generalise, typically coming out with thoughts such as, 'My best friend doesn't like me any more, no one likes me, no one ever wants to be my friend; I've never had a friendship with someone who is really sincere, and I obviously never will.'

Our thoughts when experiencing shame are self-attacking ones leading to self-disgust, self-hatred, anxiety, anger and the belief that we're failures, and they also manage to convince us that others see us as inferior, laughable, stupid or whatever we most dread their thinking. Depression makes us hard to live with and, when shame is a major problem, we are liable to handle criticism and conflicts badly – we quickly get angry, give in to avoid further argument or walk away and sulk.

Shame is not the same as guilt, which is a huge subject demanding more space than is available here. However, guilt is what we feel as a result of harming (or believing we've harmed, hurt or disappointed) another person. Shame comprises the feelings I have already outlined, of inadequacy, disgust and failure, which we direct at ourselves. Cognitive behavioural therapy can help you face and overcome feelings of shame. Meanwhile, here are some self-help tips to get recovery under way.

Challenge self-generalisations

Start with a sheet of paper and a biro, and write down everything you have been and done in the past, and then in the present, that makes you feel ashamed now. Then repeat the exercise, asking what failures from the past and present make you feel ashamed today. Read over what you have written, and watch out especially for over-generalisations and all-or-nothing thinking of the following kind: 'I am ashamed that I failed my driving test after X or Y paid for all those driving lessons. I'm obviously no good on the road, and will never make the grade.'

Challenge such over-generalisations immediately. In the above instance, for example, you would ask yourself whether your instructor would have encouraged you to enter for your test, if he/she did not think you were ready. Did you feel confident beforehand that you had a reasonable chance of getting through? Where did this confidence come from? If everyone who failed their driving test first time gave up all thoughts of driving, we'd have far fewer drivers. And examiners always give feedback. What did they praise? You'll know, of course, what you could have handled better. So you can work on it, and increase your chances of success next time. And so on . . .

Be your own best friend

Once more, be your own best friend. Think of hearing someone close to you pouring out the false beliefs of inadequacy, stupidity and being different from others that you apply to yourself. What would you say to cheer them up? First, you could rationally challenge their claims in the way described. Then you could focus on their good points (we all have them), emphasising what you love about them – things that they do or ways they behave that you like and admire. Then reassure them that you love them/feel affection for them, warts and all, and appreciate their excellent qualities. It's particularly helpful to make yourself extra comfortable physically when applying emotional balm – it's the nearest thing, if you're alone, to a warm hug and a kiss.

You can find further advice on protecting yourself from feelings of shame and other negative thoughts when we look at guilt overleaf. Meanwhile, the story Pam tells reveals the misery her shame caused her over many years.

CASE HISTORY: PAM

I'm fifty next birthday, and I was seventeen when I first suffered from depression – I had a baby at fifteen by my boyfriend from school, and we saved up for a big white wedding when Charnelle was a year old and I was six months' gone with the twins. It didn't last – Bob wouldn't work and we had to live on child benefit and other handouts. I felt so ashamed – Mum and Dad never lived off the state, and I didn't tell them for ages.

Also, Bob changed once I got pregnant for the second time. I stayed very thin – I've never put on much weight while expecting – but he hated my 'bump'. Said I looked like an old woman with middle-age spread. I also had water infections throughout the pregnancy and was too sore for love-making. So Bob told me I was not only ugly and old, but also frigid. I just felt worthless, and this reminded me of how my aunt used to make me and my sister Nancy feel when she looked after us as babies and small children.

Nancy had a nervous breakdown and was in hospital for ages. Me, I've just battled with depression and feeling inferior and different, which is what the therapist found when I first started sessions. She taught me how to get rid of unwanted thoughts, but what I found most useful were the questions she told me to ask myself, challenging all my old ideas of being inferior. It was strange at first, because I had always taken being inferior for granted, and it took six months' hard slog finally to get rid of these feelings. But I have learned to keep them at arms' length if they do threaten to return by asking *why*, exactly, I am so inferior and so much worse than other people. There aren't any real reasons, are there? And I am not. It has helped the depression so much, finally to accept this as the truth.

Guilt

We feel guilty when we are aware that we have harmed someone unjustly, or believe that we have done so. Today's society does not encourage us to experience guilt. Many of us come to believe that the rest of the world is to blame, and that it's other people's fault if they suffer for crossing us. Nevertheless, apart from psychopaths (sociopaths) who have neither consciences nor the capacity to empathise with others, we are all capable of feeling regret, remorse and, yes, a sense of guilt.

The recognition of personal guilt is, therefore, useful in that it prompts us to behave morally, and to avoid incurring bitter legacies of remorse. Yet it can be deeply destructive if it shackles us to the past, triggering caustic self-criticism leading to clinical depression. The most effective way of banishing guilty feelings is to make amends for what we have done. This is rarely easy, however. Just saying sorry can be hugely embarrassing, while physically recompensing a victim from our past may be impossible – we may not have seen them for years or, worse still, they may be dead. Talking over the event with a wise, detached friend, a minister, psychotherapist or counsellor may be the only route away from remorse to mental harmony and balance.

In the meantime, if you are weighed down by remorse, ask yourself three questions and hang on to the answers:

1. **Was I *really* to blame?** If you were – fair enough – you have made a huge stride towards banishing your misery by acknowledging responsibility. But don't be *too* hard on yourself. It's unusual for all the blame to attach to one party, leaving the other guiltless. Accept your role in the event, mentally draw a barrier around it, then ask yourself:

2. **Can I put things right?** If you can have a discussion with the person and say sorry – that's wonderful. Both of you should benefit. If they will not accept your apology – that is not your fault. At least you have tried (and may possibly try again, later on). If goods, money or other possessions played a part in your relationship, pay back what you owe – or at least make an attempt to do so. This may seem too distasteful to contemplate, but remember – you want to feel justifiably better about yourself. So be as generous as you can.

3. **Isn't it time I moved on?** I'm sure you know, in your heart of hearts, that it is. Whether or not you can make amends now, *neither the victim, nor you nor anyone else* has

anything to gain from your continuing to punish yourself. You will remain depressed, your life will remain on hold and colleagues, family and friends will inevitably suffer. Let go of your guilt and regret – if you like, using a technique described earlier (*see pages 139–42*) for banishing unwanted thoughts.

CULTIVATING POSITIVE FEELINGS

Affirmations are a brilliant way of replacing useless, destructive thoughts and feelings with healthy ones. They are positive statements that we wish to believe or to become true, and if we repeat them often enough, then they do.

You may not believe this at first – I didn't. How can we start believing that we are attractive, for instance, when we know we're overweight and spotty, or that we're a valuable, efficient job candidate when, for the past six months, we've been applying unsuccessfully for posts? Affirmations work because they act upon the subconscious mind, the repository of all our memories from babyhood to the present. The subconscious is uncritical – we can get it to accept or believe anything we choose, if we can only access it by first diverting our conscious, critical faculties.

New ideas and beliefs, of course, generate new feelings. We can alter how we feel by accepting as fact the things we wish to be true. The secret lies in the repetition, in the writing down of the affirmations, and repeating them over and over. This distracts our conscious mind (our critical disbelief faculties), which becomes bored with this 'meaningless' jingle and looks elsewhere for a focus. Affirmations are comparable in this respect to hypnotherapy, which distracts the conscious mind from the hypnotist's suggestions through the use of simple exercises – gazing at a light, perhaps, or interlocking the fingers and trying to pull them apart, or the old method of watching a swinging pendulum.

Today, many sports therapists recommend the affirmation technique to hone the confidence of their competing clients. It's essential to phrase the affirmations entirely positively, leaving out words like 'never', 'not' and 'won't'. So you would choose a sentence such as 'I am a useful, efficient clerk/care assistant/butcher's apprentice and a job will soon come my way'. You can fit affirmations into your life by:

- Saying them over and over while getting dressed, washing, making beds, peeling vegetables, filing, cleaning your teeth or whatever.
- Writing them down a set number of times daily – this is how school lines are meant to work, although tradition- ally they were expressed in negative terms unsuitable for affirmations, for example 'I must not be late for assembly.' If only teachers had known that one hundred repetitions of 'I must be in time for assembly' instead might have worked wonders!
- Writing or printing an affirmation on a piece of paper which you keep where you are bound to see it frequently throughout the evening/day – for example stuck to the edge of a mirror, or attached to fridge door or kitchen notice board.
- Recording the affirmation onto a cassette tape and listen- ing to this when convenient. (Do not try this while driving as it may cause an accident.)

Here's how Marnie used affirmations to help her overcome feelings of guilt at having been raped at the age of twelve.

CASE HISTORY: MARNIE

I am nineteen now, and I'm only just starting to feel OK around men. Dad was violent to our mum and us children when we were small, but he left home when I was five and for a long time I hardly thought about him. Then, when I was twelve, Mum had a letter from Dad's brother Fred, telling us that Dad had passed away in prison, and asking if Fred could come and see us. Mum said yes, and it turned out that Fred had just moved to our area – after a four-year prison sentence for downloading (and selling) child pornography over the Internet.

He was nice as pie at first – good clothes, took Mum and us kids out, bought us things. My sisters and I thought he was cool. Even our older brother started to come round, although he had hated our dad and was very protective of Mum. Fred worked as a bricklayer and hod carrier on a building site; he'd do tons of overtime and get a load of money, then have a few weeks off and spend it all – often on our family.

I was tall for twelve years of age – five feet, six inches, and well developed. My youngest sister and I used to play dressing up in clothes Mum got from Oxfam for us – often Fred would come in while we were changing and look at us in a funny way. We weren't used to having a dad around, so we just thought it was normal. Then one day a week after my birthday, Fred came round when I was off school with tonsillitis. Mum was at work. Fred said something about dressing up for him, but I didn't feel well and told him no. He started to breathe funnily – really noisy breathing – and his eyes went glassy and started to stare. I was frightened – I thought he was having some sort of attack.

He went into the bathroom but came out after a few minutes wearing my brother's dressing gown. I asked him if he were going to have a bath, and he said, 'Yes, if you come and watch me.' I knew that was out of order – the idea made me feel horrible – so I ran into my bedroom and tried to lock the door. Fred was too strong for me – he pushed me onto the bed, pulled off my track-suit bottoms and raped me on the floor – twice, once in the vagina and once in my bottom.

It was terrifying and agonisingly painful. I'd only kissed a boy twice, and we never went any further. Fred was like a disgusting great farm animal – grunting and shoving and sweating – then getting up and wiping himself with my trackies. He shook his finger in my face – said he'd tell Mum and get me taken into care if I told anyone. Then he poured himself a glass of Mum's Christmas whisky and went away.

Mum and I had always been very close – she'd done a good job protecting us from Dad when he was around, and there was no way I could keep something like that to myself. All the same, I felt so guilty and dirty, I was hysterical when I rang her at her office. She came straight home, listened to what had happened and took me to the police station. I had showered before we got there but we had the tracksuit bottoms as evidence. The case came to court, and Fred was sentenced to twelve years' imprisonment.

I knew it wasn't my fault – Mum and the police told me so over and over, but I always felt at fault, and as though I was somehow to blame. I did have some counselling but the counsellor moved away after a month and I didn't like the one who took her place. I had no interest in boys, and I started to get very depressed – failed my GCEs, cried a lot, wouldn't go out with my friends. Then I took a temporary factory job and met Joe, my boyfriend. I couldn't let him touch me for ages, but he was very patient – he'd been depressed himself in the past and had been taught about affirmations to combat nasty thoughts and feelings.

I just did what Joe suggested, because I trusted him. My first affirmation was 'I am feeling better and better about myself every day.' It sounded daft at first, because I didn't feel anything of the sort, but after six weeks or so, I started to feel this way. Then we tried other ones, a bit nearer the mark – 'I am guilt-free and a good, attractive person' progressing to 'The rape is over and done with, and I have grown from my experience.' Shortly afterwards, Joe and I asked for a referral for psychosexual counselling, which has also done a lot of good. We can make love now and I can actually enjoy it. I've been free of depression, too, for over a year.

In the final chapter, we will look at how relaxation can soothe the tension and anxiety that depression-linked stress can cause, and enhance all the treatments and self-help techniques you've read about so far.

CHAPTER 8

Relaxation Techniques

Relaxation in some form is essential to life. Severe, prolonged stress from which it was impossible to retreat would cause physical and mental collapse, followed by death from a heart attack or a stroke. As it is, over-stimulation of the pituitary and hypothalamus in the brain, and of the adrenal glands under their control, elevates blood levels of adrenaline and nora-drenaline and destroys mood-raising serotonin. Depression and tension inevitably follow, together with anxiety-linked disorders such as phobias, uncontrolled worry, tension headaches and insomnia, and more obviously life-threatening complaints, such as cancer, heart disease and premature ageing.

We cannot help but be aware of this, at some level. Stress is perennially newsworthy, and official figures released in March 2004 showed a record figure of nearly a million Britons claiming incapacity benefit for mental and behavioural disorders precipitated by stress. Moreover, however healthy we believe ourselves to be, we all experience the ill effects of stress at some time. Despite this, there is a certain amount of resistance to the suggestion that we should relax more. Men are less inclined than women to accept suggestions for regular, planned relaxation, and both sexes tend to claim that they lack the time. Some say they are unable to relax while being unwilling to try, and many fear that (like depression) stress symptoms will be misconstrued as weakness.

The fact is that nearly everyone can learn to switch off. Some of us are better at it than others, but it's a tool we all need if we're to combat unwanted illnesses and optimise our energy and well-being. Sleep, concentration and mental performance all benefit. Here is a relaxation technique for regular practice and use.

DEEP MUSCULAR RELAXATION

This method shows you what muscular tension feels like, and how a few simple steps can reverse its unpleasant sensation. It consists of contracting, then relaxing muscle groups throughout the body – it is usually recommended to start with the feet and legs, and work up the body to the neck, head, scalp, face and tongue. Feeling tense all over can become so habitual that we cease to notice it. Focusing on a 'squeeze and relax' routine reminds us what muscular tension feels like, and points to the muscles needing special attention. It also distracts us from distressing or negative repetitive thoughts and, by soothing the body, helps to calm the mind.

Wear loose, comfortable clothing when doing this exercise – a tracksuit is ideal. Sit in a comfortable chair or lie on a rug on the floor. Try to ensure that you will be left quietly alone for twenty to thirty minutes at least, and to start with, turn off the radio, TV or other noise sources. Later, you may choose to play peaceful, gentle music as a relaxation aid.

The basic routine is the same for all the muscle groups:

- Tense and hold for fifteen to twenty seconds – note how this feels.
- Say 'relax' to yourself and let the tension go.

- Focus on the difference in feeling between the two states. Enjoy the sensation for twenty to thirty seconds, repeat if necessary and move on to another group.

Focus on these muscle groups in turn:

Legs and feet

Work on each side in turn.

- **Toes/feet** Curl your toes – not hard enough to give you cramp, but hard enough to feel the pull. Then uncurl and move on.

- **Lower legs** Bend your toes and feet downwards and squeeze, tightening the calf muscles; next, bend your toes and feet upwards towards your face, tightening the muscles at the fronts and sides. Relax.

- **Thighs** Straighten and stiffen your legs, bringing your feet slightly upwards to tense muscles at the front, then bend slightly at the knees to flex the muscles on the backs of thighs. Then relax.

Trunk

- **Stomach** Pull in your stomach, and then push it out.

- **Buttocks** Squeeze and relax.

- **Back** Arch, and relax.

- **Chest** Take a deep breath and hold it, then let it go and relax.

Arms and hands

Do each of the following in turn. Relax.

- **Hands and forearms** Make a tight fist, and bend your forearms downwards at the elbows. Relax.

- **Biceps (fronts of upper arms)** Make a 'muscle' on both your arms. Relax.

- **Triceps (backs of upper arms)** Stretch your arms out straight, and tense the backs of your upper arms. Relax.

Upper body

- **Shoulders** Shrug your shoulders and roll them backwards and forwards. Let your shoulders sag.

- **Neck** Roll your head right around in a circle, up over your right shoulder, downwards, up over your left shoulder and upwards to the ceiling or the floor above your head.

- **Jaws** Clench your jaws, then let go.

- **Forehead** Frown hard, then raise your eyebrows. Relax.

- **Lips** Press your lips together, then relax.

- **Tongue** Stick out your tongue, then put it in and press it against the roof of your mouth. Relax.

Total body relaxation

- Check each muscle group in turn, and repeat the tensing/letting go routine for any group as required.

- Tell yourself that you feel warm, comfortable and relaxed all over.

- Imagine that you are floating gently down a perfumed stream strewn with rose petals.

- Count down slowly from 10 to 1, enjoying the dappled sunlight, the shade, the birds and the flowers. You are feeling more and more deeply relaxed as you approach a small, secret pool where you come gently to rest, perfectly relaxed and at peace.

- Enjoy your time in the secret pool.

- When you wish to come out of this state, say to yourself: 'To wake up, I am going to count from 1 to 10. By the time I reach ten, I shall be wide awake and refreshed. 1 . . . 2 . . . 3 . . . 4 . . . 5 . . . I am waking up . . . 6 . . . 7 . . . 8 . . . I am stretching and opening my eyes . . . 9 . . . 10 . . . I am fully awake and feeling wonderful.'

ANOTHER RELAXATION METHOD

I have devised an alternative relaxation method that is equally simple to use. It happens to work slightly more quickly, but its purpose (second to pleasure) is the reassuring, tangible proof of the mind's powerful control over the body. In this instance, the sensations result from the interplay between the (inhibiting) conscious mind, and the suggestibility of the subconscious.

Lie or sit comfortably as before. Once you are calm and still, concentrate on one of your feet – let's say the right one. Try to contract its muscles – squeezing the toes, bending the foot downwards, and so on – but at the same time, prevent any movement from actually taking place. I say to myself: 'I am squeezing my (right) foot – but I can't do so. I am squeezing as hard as I can – but nothing is happening.' You will feel a sort of warm vibration passing through the body area on which you are concentrating, as though all the tiny fibres in the targeted muscles are contracting randomly on their own, instead of concertedly, leaving the muscle as a whole immobile.

Then do the same with your left foot, then right calf, left calf, right then left thigh, buttocks, then stomach muscles and so on, working up your body as before and ending with your tongue. The higher up your body you move, the fainter the trembly, vibratory sensation will become. This doesn't matter:

having achieved the sensation in your feet and lower legs (and possibly your thighs), each part in turn will become relaxed. It takes me about six to seven minutes to relax in this way and, when I have done so, I repeat calming words or a phrase, drawing them out like this: 'Relaaaaax . . .' 'Peeeaaaaace, be stiiiiill . . . ' 'Total caaaaalm . . . ' You can choose your own words and will, I hope, enjoy this method.

RELAXING IN A MOMENT

Regular relaxation makes it easier to deal with negative stress generally; but what do we do when we're suddenly faced with a stressful situation at work, at home, in a shop, at the bank, or – the two worst situations of all – when we're driving or trying to cope with automated telephone systems? For some of us, a couple of seconds is all it takes for our blood pressure to zoom upwards, for angry words or tears to escape, and for scalding steam to start pouring out of our ears. Here is a method of achieving calm in the face of intolerable emotion.

Firstly, take two or three very slow, very deep breaths – this will slow your heart rate and quell some of the adrenaline effects. Then sit down (even if you have to go to the loo, or into the utility room, a garden or a shed – sit down *somewhere* as comfortably as you can), and make use of just a small part of your total body relaxation routine. Make a tight fist with your right hand, say, squeeze for a second or two and feel the tightness in your hand, wrist and forearm. Then, gently, relax. Say the words as you do the actions, 'Teeeense . . . relaaaaax,' in the gentle, drawn-out way you have used before.

Now 'make a muscle' with your biceps, and again, still breathing slowly and deeply, say the words, 'Teeeeense . . . relaaaaax.' Feel the tightness in the front of your upper arm, followed by the loose, limp sensation of relaxation. Then straighten your arm at the elbow, and squeeze all the muscles as hard as you can without hurting yourself – saying as you do so, 'Teeeeense . . . relaaaaax.'

You can prepare for doing this exercise at a time of stress by first rehearsing it straight after a normal relaxation session: picture something that normally stresses you getting squeezed into the tightness of your fist, your biceps, your whole arm muscles, following each tense squeeze with completely loose, limp, floppy relaxation. The passing of the tension out of each muscle group, symbolises – *or rather is* – the draining away of your anger, fear, frustration or other negative feeling.

When you really cannot leave the room, store or wherever, you can make do (quite nicely) with a single clenched fist – it should be clenched as tightly as you can manage, and for a fairly prolonged period. Drive all your negative emotion down into the iron-hard muscles and release it, letting it trickle away as you relax. Repeat the words to go with the action under your breath, or just say them in your mind.

AUTOHYPNOSIS

A further relaxation technique utilises what hypnotherapists call 'arm levitation'. It's a novel experience. They sometimes use it to demonstrate the power of hypnosis to new clients (making their arm rise up without effort on their part, at the suggestion of the therapist); it's a bit of a novelty, and really quite impressive, and it also tests the client's suggestibility (that is, their susceptibility) to hypnotic suggestion.

The same technique can also be used as a form of auto-hypnosis. I try it out sometimes when I can't go to sleep, and it certainly passes a few minutes usefully in preparing for slumber. I have never experienced anything but beneficial effects from it, either personally or with clients, although some experts claim that it (and other relaxation methods) can trigger panic attacks in unusually sensitive people. If you do suffer with your nerves – experience panic attacks, palpitations,

sweating and other anxiety symptoms, or become easily hysterical when stressed – it would be better to consult your doctor
or a qualified hypnotherapist before embarking on this or any
other sort of autohypnosis technique.

This is how it's done. Lie comfortably, with your legs
stretched out, your ankles slightly apart, and your arms and
hands stretched out and lying still on either side of your body.
Make yourself as relaxed and comfortable as possible, then
concentrate on one of your hands. Clench and relax the hand
a few times, concentrating upon achieving complete relaxation in its every part.

Then, when your hand is truly as limp and 'lifeless' as you
can make it, say 'My (left) hand is starting to rise. Very, very
slowly, without any effort from me, my left hand is slowly
and surely starting to lift up – a helium balloon is attached
to my wrist, and is slowly but surely carrying my hand
upwards without my conscious effort. Slowly but surely,
slowly but surely, my left hand is rising from the [floor, bed,
sofa, my lap or whatever]; it's as light as a feather, as light
as gossamer, up it goes – upwards, upwards, upwards . . .'

You are instructing your subconscious mind to carry out an
action that you have prohibited your conscious mind from
performing. You will probably notice a similar warm, vibratory feeling in your hand muscles to the one described in the
last exercise. And if you increase the intensity of your suggestions – repeating them over and over, saying them more and
more emphatically as the thumb and fingers start to twitch
and then move, you will find that your hand – and possibly
your entire arm – will slowly rise upwards until it is anything
from a fraction of a centimetre above the surface on which it
has been resting, to extended fully above your head, suspended
in the air without any conscious effort on your part.

With your hand and arm aloft, you can then imagine that
you are floating down a stream or, say, on a cloud down a
mountainside (or whatever), and prolong the relaxation for

fifteen to twenty minutes if you wish. When you are ready to end your relaxation session, you will feel normal muscular power return and you can bring your arm and hand down gently.

Here's how hypnotherapy helped Dodo, in her own words.

CASE HISTORY: DODO

I tried very hard to overcome my depression after my sister died. We were twins – not identical, but we couldn't have been closer if we had been. We were fifty-seven when Deirdre was diagnosed with breast cancer, and at first the reality failed to hit us. You see, nothing had ever happened to either of us that we couldn't defeat together. I realise now that Deirdre believed that I would be able to make everything right for her. I was the elder by twelve minutes! We were worried by the diagnosis, of course, but neither of us considered the possibility of her dying. I certainly didn't.

Then she was sent for a body scan after her chemotherapy and radiotherapy came to an end. I'd been there throughout for her – we shared a house, and neither of us ever married – and we had even planned a celebration with our younger brother and his family for the day the result was due. The scan revealed that there were secondary cancers in her spine and skull, and the consultant told her that she had less than six months to live.

Of course, we cancelled the dinner. From then onwards, it was Deirdre keeping my spirits up, instead of the other way around. She was not afraid of dying – we've always gone to church, and believed in an afterlife, but I just couldn't face the idea of life without her. Actually, we beat the prognosis, but only by a month. By Christmas that year, Deirdre was dead, and I was suffering such terrible depression that all I wanted to do was to die. I didn't try to kill myself – but I often felt like doing so. I couldn't eat or sleep, I cried all the time – all day, every day. I only went out to the corner shop, and three times a week to visit Deirdre's grave. Then my brother Darrell, who lives 200 miles away, came round. He had tried repeatedly to contact me, but I hadn't returned his letters or calls.

As soon as Darrell saw how distraught I was he rang our doctor. She visited that day, and easily persuaded me to go into hospital; I felt like death, and was totally compliant. I simply didn't care what happened to me, or to anyone else. I stayed in the hospital for nearly two months; I was given electroconvulsive therapy and an antidepressant, both of which helped me to feel human again. When I was about to be discharged, the consultant psychiatrist mentioned that hypnotherapy might help me. He knew I had problems with relaxation and sleep, and put me in touch with a therapist in my area.

Deirdre and I were always open-minded about alternative treatments – although hypnotherapy is pretty mainstream, now. The therapist taught me to relax, and to repeat positive suggestions to myself once I had reached a relaxed state. I had to say, 'I am at peace. All the muscles of my body are limp, loose, floppy and relaxed. I can now love Deirdre as I always have, but without this harming my life. From now, I shall go from strength to strength – for her sake and for mine.'

At first it was hard because, being depressed, I lacked motivation but, as I went on with the tablets at home, I could see more and more point in trying to come to terms with Deirdre's death. I had always been a worrier – as had Deirdre – something we inherited from our mother. But I have practised deep-muscle relaxation daily ever since, and am now getting a life of my own again . . .

YOGA

You may find the notion of yoga offputting if you doubt the need for relaxation in the first place. True, it evokes memories of flower power and crystal-waving hippies, but fortunately for its image (and for us), yoga has become ever more widely accepted since the 1960s. In fact, it is difficult to find a leisure centre, evening class programme or fitness group in most countries in the West where it fails to figure among the most eagerly subscribed topics.

As you probably know, yoga originated in India and, although we are considering it here as a source of relaxation training, it is a very great deal more besides. In fact, a description of some of its exercises falls far short of accounting for the profound relaxation it can bring. It can work on depression on so many levels that I am giving a brief sketch of the basic ideas on which it is founded.

Yoga means 'union' – not, traditionally, of body, mind and spirit, although its harmonising effects in this respect account for much of its popularity – but of man's individual consciousness (known as Jivatman) and the universal consciousness (Paramatman). So 'yoga' implies both an altered state of awareness (as does deep relaxation), *and* the means by which this can be achieved. Many of yoga's fundamental beliefs originated in the Indian subcontinent a very long time before being 'discovered' in the West. The European concept of universal consciousness, for instance, entered our literature in psychoanalyst Carl Jung's writings during the twentieth century. Yet yogis (those who practise yoga) were aware of the universal mind – and how to unite with it, experiencing bliss – at least 5,000 years before the birth of Christ.

The early yoga teachers also formulated and passed down in their teachings their perception of what quantum physicists today call the unified field – the ultimate state of being for all matter, energy and motion, a complex interplay of vibratory electromagnetic fields. If anything can reassure us of the wisdom of the ancient Indian sages, who made these deductions millennia before scientific investigation came into being, this surely must.

Yoga lays down guidelines for five essential practices – proper exercise, proper breathing, proper relaxation, proper diet and positive thinking/meditation. Traditionally, these have been classified into four paths (Margas) – Jnana yoga (the yoga of wisdom that develops the intellect), Bhakti yoga (the yoga of devotion that opens the heart), Karma yoga (the yoga of action and of selfless service) and Raja yoga, the royal or psychological path involving the mind. Hatha yoga, one of the most popular forms practised in Britain today, paves the way to the more advanced stages of Raja yoga.

Swami Sivananda, a world-renowned guru of the late nineteenth and early twentieth centuries, recognised that we can all identify with each of these elements – intellect, heart, body and mind – and suggested that yogis should practise techniques from each of them. This is now known as Sivananda yoga or the yoga of synthesis. He also taught that we should be free to follow one path rather than another, according to our needs and temperaments.

Yogic exercises are intended to develop our bodies and, partly through this development, our mental and spiritual faculties. Yogic asanas, meaning 'steady poses', form the basis of yoga for all of us, as beginners. Practising them regularly improves the flexibility, health and strength of the spine, in order to maintain an adequate circulation of blood, oxygen and nutrients to the spinal cord, brain and peripheral nerves (nerves travelling from the brain and spinal cord to other body areas). Many of the asanas also strengthen and help to balance the body's stress-control systems, such as the pituitary and other endocrine glands, and the adrenals, which can go into overdrive when we're under strain or are having to deal with uncontrollable stress.

Eight million, four hundred thousand asanas are said to be mentioned in the ancient religious texts, but there are twelve basic ones learned and practised for everyday relaxation and benefit. Their names are literal or figurative descriptions of the shapes our bodies assume when we do them: they comprise headstand, shoulder stand, plough, fish, forward bend, cobra, locust, bow, spinal twist, crow pose, standing forward bend and triangle. At the end of a practice sessions, you have to do a deeper final relaxation called the corpse.

The corpse is also a logical conclusion to the other relaxation exercises described in this chapter, and helps the practitioner to reap the benefits of all that has gone before. This is how to do it.

The corpse

Lie on your back with your feet at least 18in (45cm) apart, and allowing the toes to fall outwards to the side. Place your arms at an angle of about forty-five degrees to your body and relax your hands, allowing your fingers to curl gently. Breathe regularly and gently.

- Go through one of the 'tense and relax' routines already described.

- Then, starting with your toes, sense a wave of relaxation moving slowly up through your whole body. In your mind, relax each toe, followed by each foot.

- Feel the relaxation creeping up your legs, relaxing your calves, knees and thighs. Feel the relaxation wave entering your hips and pelvic region. Mentally relax all the internal organs of this region.

- Relax your buttocks and feel the tension drifting out of every part of your back. Think that the floor is holding you up – as your body becomes more deeply relaxed, you feel as though you are sinking down into the floor.

- Feel the relaxation wave reaching your chest, as you continue breathing gently and slowly and regularly.

- Concentrate and relax each finger in turn, then each hand. Feel the relaxation creeping up your arms, relaxing your wrists, forearms, elbows and upper arms.

- Relax your shoulders, and feel the wave of relaxation moving up your neck and into your scalp and head.

- Relax your face and scalp muscles – start with your jaw and let your mouth hang slightly open.

- Relax your tongue and the muscles at the back of your mouth and throat. Relax your chin and your cheeks, eyes and eyebrows, forehead and scalp.

- Lastly, relax your brain. All cares and anxieties have melted away like a patch of snow in the sun. Remain in this state of relaxation for at least five minutes.

Here is how Michelle experienced yoga when she took it up to help her relax:

CASE HISTORY: MICHELLE

I was nineteen when I lost the baby. Me and Derek had been going out for a month – he worked as a bouncer in the nightclub where I was a hostess, and we had an accident with a condom. I didn't really think about it much – it had happened before. But I noticed from my diary a couple of days afterwards that we'd had sex around the middle of my cycle, so I was a bit concerned . . .

When I found I was expecting, I texted Derek but he didn't reply. He was already going out with my mate so I thought I'd keep the baby just to spite him. Wasn't the right attitude, I know that. Then, three weeks before the baby was due, I got drunk and fell down the stairs at my mum's. My little boy was born in hospital by emergency Caesarean a couple of hours later – but it was too late. I had suffered internal bruising and he had severe brain damage and they couldn't start off his breathing when he was delivered.

That's when it hit me. I hadn't thought of him as a person till then. My mum and sister both have three kids all by different dads, and I didn't think being pregnant was that important. But when I realised I had lost something that might really have loved me and needed me, I was heartbroken. I cried and cried, and lost interest in my mates and going out. I couldn't work and lost my job, and I hurt all over. I felt like a murderer. The doctor said it wasn't just the fall, it was the shock, and that I was also depressed.

I saw a counsellor, which helped a bit, but I got very jumpy and nervy, still cried a lot and couldn't relax. The first antidepressant the doctor gave me made me sick. But he changed it and that helped – although I still had horrible thoughts all the time, and couldn't sit still or relax at all.

I was at my doctor's when I picked up a leaflet in the waiting room about yoga. I'd heard of it, though it wasn't something I'd ever thought of doing. But the locum I saw, a lady doctor, was all for it. She said it had helped her after she lost one of her twins at birth. So I decided to give it a go. The classes were held twice a week at the local leisure centre. I started and really enjoyed it. I told the teacher I couldn't do all the movements at first because of the bruising to my spine, but she was very helpful and told me specially, each time one came up that would be bad for me, what to do instead. Before long I had got my strength back and could do most of the asanas.

The best thing was being able to do them at home. I finished each exercise session with the corpse, and would go off into a lovely, dreamy state, imagining a tide of warm, gentle water lapping at my body and helping me relax. I found I could switch on a feeling of relaxation whenever I wanted to – I just had to close my eyes for a second or two, and sense warm, comforting water creeping up, like a bath. I started to sleep better, and the worrying thoughts went away, too. Now I am doing an advanced yoga course and am going to train as a yoga teacher. So good did come of my pregnancy and accident in the end, in a funny sort of way.

T'AI CHI

T'ai chi, also known as t'ai chi ch'uan, or taijiquan, is an extremely appealing, restful and balancing method of learning (among other things) to relax, and of establishing harmony between body, mind and spirit. In Australia and California it is often taught and practised out of doors, and films about China, Thailand and other Far Eastern countries frequently show everyday citizens performing t'ai chi in public.

T'ai chi is an ancient Chinese system of co-ordinated body movements used to promote mental and physical health, and also to provide effective self-defence (the latter aim need not concern us here). T'ai chi exemplifies holism in action, focusing as it does upon the enhancement of chi, or qi, the body's internal energy (which Western complementary practitioners refer to as vitality, or the life force). Its object is to achieve balance through rhythmic, soft movements that are both purposeful and relaxed and that, when performed correctly, give the impression of continuity and ease.

The elements of t'ai chi are not difficult to learn, and they are relaxing and rewarding since you feel that you are making progress quite early on. It is a unique art, which demands much patient practice before one can become truly competent at it. The appearance of continuity it gives results from a series of movement routines with names such as grasp sparrow tail, which the body stance and limb movements mimic. These flow into one another according to a predetermined pattern, and result in an impressive and visually beautiful sequence that looks, to a beginner, like a mixture of stretch exercises and dancing.

Besides relaxation, this method of cultivating chi increases energy, strength and health, and improves tolerance and self-confidence. It does not rely on speed, strength or force, which makes it suitable for most people, from small children to elderly people. In many ways, t'ai chi is ideal for depression sufferers because its movements are relatively undemanding. Like yoga, it is non-competitive, and learning it should never give rise to anxiety or strain. On the contrary, t'ai chi improves our ability to handle stress, at the same time toning the muscles and improving co-ordination, posture and balance (which in turn boosts self-esteem after, perhaps, a long period of depressed inactivity).

Other reported health benefits of t'ai chi include a reduction in blood pressure, better digestion and circulation, and more freedom from joint stiffness and muscular pain in people with mild arthritis and other, similar conditions. Here is a specific tension-dispersing technique called the shower, which you can do sitting down.

The shower

Kneel or sit down with your feet firmly on the ground, and picture yourself taking a shower. Adjust the temperature and pressure of the water to your liking; you may fancy a short, sharp blast of icy water 'needles' on your upper back to energise you and wake you up. If you are feeling a bit fragile, though, a comforting, warm shower may be more suitable. Sit or kneel quietly under your imaginary shower, letting your mind drift gently as the stresses of the day are washed away.

This is the story of Charlie, who took up t'ai chi after a car accident.

CASE HISTORY: CHARLIE

I'm twenty-eight now, and the accident happened three years ago, just after I'd asked Melanie to marry me. In fact, we were on our way to our engagement party in my new company car, and a security van turned out of a side street right in front of us. I couldn't avoid hitting him, but I braked very hard and swerved, hitting a lamp post. The van driver was all right – just put his foot down and sped off. We had no chance to take his number. I was concussed and spent the night in hospital, while Melanie had quite severe whiplash injury to her neck and upper back.

I'd been driving for seven years at the time of the accident, and had had the odd scrape before, but this one really shook me up. I kept thinking how easily we might have been killed. I started to go to work by train, and made excuses for not using the car. Worries about driving again kept going round and round in my head during the day, and were keeping me awake at night.

I'd had depression in my teens, and wasn't keen to go back and discuss my feelings with our new doctor, but my mother persuaded me to go and see him. He advised me to stave off another depression attack by taking some positive action and learning to relax. My younger sister had taken up t'ai chi a few months earlier, and she suggested I go to the beginners' class. She assured me that it wasn't just for women; at least half the people in my class were men – some my age, but there was also a young lad of sixteen and a much older man of around seventy.

I had always been interested in the martial arts, so I understood some of the thinking behind t'ai chi, but this was completely non-aggressive. Our teacher, a Chinese man called Mr Tan, explained that the movements can be adapted to self-defence, but that our purpose in his classes was solely to improve our inner harmony, energy and balance. Mr Tan taught us the opening movements of 'drawing in chi' – gathering the life force into the chest area – and enhancing its strength throughout the body by a sequence of body positions and arm and leg movements.

I liked the fact that we learned one t'ai chi sequence at a time thoroughly before going on to the next. This made it easy to practise at home, and I started doing a few minutes every day. I think it was the sense of controlled power and balance that t'ai chi gave me, plus the philosophy behind it, that I found so appealing. Anyway, its soothing effects enabled me to conquer my nerves and start driving again. I persuaded Melanie to come to classes, too, once her doctor agreed that it was safe to do so. She found that the exercises eased her stress, and helped her muscles and joints regain strength and balance. We both do it every day now, because we enjoy it so much.

MEDITATION

Meditation calms the body and mind, and brings about a change in consciousness which, when carried out successfully, leads to a sense of blissful calm that enables you to deal with the most adverse circumstances without becoming depressed or stressed. This goal can take some time to reach: like every other skill, meditation becomes easier and more productive with practice. Nevertheless, the good thing about it is that it conveys *some* benefits from the day you start including it in your daily routine, and its effects are cumulative. Several meditation methods exist. I discuss two I am familiar with, and that I know work.

Simple meditation

All meditation aims to abstract the 'self' from conscious thought. What this means is that although you remain fully conscious and aware while you are practising it, you are free of those thoughts that persistently present themselves to us throughout our waking hours. The brain functions electrically in cycles of specific wavelengths (depending upon our mood, whether we are asleep or awake, our immediate stimuli and other factors). This activity can be observed by means of an electroencephalograph (EEG), which records tracings on a screen and a paper printout like an electro-cardiograph (ECG) tracing of the electrical activity of the heart.

The point of banishing familiar everyday mental activity is to achieve brain function at certain wavelengths at which the mind is at its most effective. Problems and vexations appear in proportion, and benefits at both the rational and emotional/spiritual levels ensue: you realise that, ultimately, trivial troubles are insignificant, and also *feel* far less stressed by them. Daydreaming is a halfway step between normal consciousness and the meditative state, involving 'alpha' brain waves of ten cycles per second, enabling you to draw on 'faculties other than the five senses' – it has been suggested that through its practice you develop your innate 'sixth sense' instincts, such as clairvoyance. You also deal far more efficiently with daily anxieties, and benefit from better sleep and fewer stress-related complaints, such as migraines, tension headaches and stomach upsets. Here is how to go about a simple meditation session.

- Set aside thirty minutes of your day when you will be alone, and can unplug the telephone and maybe leave a note on your front door saying that you do not wish to be disturbed between X and Y hours.

- Have a shower or bath if you have time, and put on some simple and undemanding clothes that make you feel relaxed and at ease.

- Sit down on a floor cushion or on a straight-backed chair, in a dimly lit room with all possible noise quelled – at least to start with. You can light a candle, if you wish, and warm some soothing aromatherapy oil of your choice (*see pages 111–16*) in an oil heater.

- Sit comfortably and breathe deeply and slowly – if you have time, you could use one of the relaxation methods outlined earlier (*see page 153*).

- Feel and hear the breath slowly entering your body, hold for a few seconds and exhale slowly. Concentrate on just how your chest and lungs feel as you breathe. If other thoughts arise, acknowledge them and let them go. The harder you try to banish them, the longer they will stick around. Just concentrate on the *in* breath, the *holding* of the breath, and the *exhaling*. Notice how calm and free you feel, and how thoughts slowly start to disappear.

- Hold this state for as long as you can – the length of time will surely increase as you persist with your practice.

You will know when you have had enough – try to aim for ten minutes at first and gradually increase this to twenty minutes daily.

TRANSCENDENTAL MEDITATION (TM)

This is practised worldwide by more than five million people in 108 countries on all six continents, and has been researched in nearly 600 studies. It was introduced by Maharishi Mahesh Yogi in 1957 as the quintessence of ancient Vedic wisdom, which he had acquired over years of study in the Himalayas under his Master Shri Guru Dev. Practitioners express TM's purpose as the direct experience and utilisation of the field of pure being, the transcendental field of existence at the basis of everything in the universe.

The philosophy underlying Vedic wisdom can be difficult for Westerners to grasp, but it has been described in a number of books, including Maharishi Mahesh Yogi's *Science of Being and Art of Living* published in 1963. It is not essential to understand this philosophy in order to meditate the TM way, but (in a way, and this is my own analogy) not to do so is a little like going into a sweet shop blindfolded and expecting to derive satisfaction and enjoyment from the experience. If we don't know what the concepts involve, we are unlikely to be motivated to pursue them – or might be put off by a trifling difficulty instead of fixing our sight on our main objective.

Pure being, as described by Maharishi and by Vedic seers through the ages, corresponds exactly with the unified field of natural law that has been the greatest focus of theoretical physicists since the 1990s (*see also* yoga, *page 162*). The only difference between them is their range of application – the unified field remains, for the time being, a mathematical abstraction, while Maharishi and Vedic literature regard it as the most important discovery ever made, highly relevant to life today and capable of access by anyone, anywhere, at any time.

Regular practice of TM allows us to access an advanced state of meditation, confirmed in numerous studies to involve slower brain waves of five cycles per second. The practical advantages of TM are greatly increased happiness, creativity, intelligence and organisational skills; the spiritual benefit is the experience of absolute bliss. This technique has an excellent record in combating depression, and offers rich rewards for the time and persistence invested in it.

Meditation can be a hard, slow process, involving powers of concentration few of us possess, and it is therefore unlikely to be attempted – or, at any rate, sustained – by busy, stressed people living ordinary lives. However, Maharishi (and Vedic writings) reveal that the nature of the inner life of every person is bliss, and one that it is the birthright of us all to experience.

TM technique is taught through personal instruction by specially trained teachers, and consists of a seven-step programme lasting about an hour and a half a day, over the course of a week. A lot of the philosophy and background are explained, and there is as much chance as one needs to ask, question and debate the issues that arise. One does have to pay – it may differ regionally, but it cost me £500 when I learned TM while living in north Cornwall three years ago. It's made a huge difference to my life, mood control and ability to cope with uncontrollable stress. Its health benefits are legendary – it reduces blood pressure, for example, and the risks of life-threatening events, such as coronaries and strokes, are significantly reduced.

In a nutshell, you are taught, or rather given, a personal mantra to use in meditation – and plenty of practice and encouragement to ensure you are using the technique correctly. The word chosen for a candidate by their teacher is not revealed to others, and is of ancient Sanskrit origin – a 'word of power', if you like, which is sonorous and calming and, according to my teacher, with a potent energy charge instrumental in bringing the consciousness change and blissful experience intended. Mine certainly works for me.

Here is Brenda's story. She took up TM at the age of fifty.

CASE HISTORY: BRENDA

You might think that I was an obvious candidate for a meditation programme because, until I took up TM two years ago, I had been a nun in an enclosed order for thirty years. I thought I knew all I needed to know about praying and meditating – not that they're the same thing, but both of course are devotional practices and raise one's consciousness. Then our convent closed – the community fought for two years against this happening, but convents have been disappearing rapidly in Britain since the 1970s, and we could not stem the tide.

I was depressed and saddened when I came out, finding myself in a strange, alien world that it was very difficult to adjust to. I still had, and have, my faith, but I felt let down and abandoned, as did many of the sisters. My parents had died during my twenties, and my sister really didn't want to know me – although we were brought up in the same way, going to the same convent schools, she thought I was weird, wanting to enter a convent. I tried to establish a friendship with her – we'd exchanged Christmas cards while I was in the order – but there was really no common ground when I found myself in ordinary life again.

I finally went to see my doctor because I knew the symptoms of depression and believed I had them. He tried to be helpful, poor man, but I think he was out of his depth. I mean, how many abandoned nuns does the average GP get to see in the course of his practice?

He gave me a prescription for antidepressant tablets and, just as I was going into the chemist to get them, I saw a notice in the window about meditation. I phoned and they were very friendly

– they weren't TM people themselves, but we had a long chat and the woman I spoke to advised me to try TM. I thought that was very nice of her!

I had bought myself a small computer and was getting used to the Internet, so I was able to trace a local teacher quite easily. She, Chrissy, was so easy to talk to and seemed to radiate the calmness that I had once known myself. I did the course and have meditated using the TM method every day since.

It's made all the difference in the world. I can see that upsets (such as those that I had experienced) are just that – hiccups in the overall plan of things that we can cope with easily if we have inner strength and can attain genuine joy in spite of life and its trials. I have made many friends through TM and thank God for leading me to it. I never did go back to collect the antidepressants.

In this chapter we have looked at several methods of relaxing – some of these you can teach yourself, others you can learn in a class or from a videotape; all of them can be carried out alone or in a group. Relaxation should benefit body, mind and spirit, so if you really crave some personal space, choose a solitary relaxation mode instead of joining a class. Relaxation is like physical exercise – it needs to be practised regularly if you are to obtain lasting benefits, and 'little and often' is always preferable to long sessions carried out on impulse. Ideally, I would recommend twenty minutes of relaxation daily, five or six times a week, or daily if you can manage it. You will find a list of resources, including useful book titles, addresses and websites, overleaf.

The most important points to reiterate at the end of this book – ones I really want you to take to heart – are that depression is a valid, chemical illness undeserving of stigma; that though you feel isolated, you are *not* alone; and that the methods I have described can, and do, bring tangible, lasting relief. I look forward very much to them doing that for you.

Resources

FURTHER READING

Aromatherapy: An A–Z, Patricia Davis, The C. W. Daniel Company Ltd, 1995.

A Woman in Your Own Right, Anne Dickson, Quartet Books, 1982.

Effortless Exercise, Dr Caroline Shreeve, Sheldon Books, 2003.

Feel The Fear And Do It Anyway, Susan Jeffers, Rider, 1997.

Feeling Good – The New Mood Therapy, David D. Burns, MD, Avon Books, 1999.

Flower Remedies, Christine Wildwood, Robson Books, 2002.

Mind, Body and Immunity, Rachel Charles, Methuen, 1990.

Natural Highs, Patrick Holford and Dr Hyla Cass, Piatkus Books, 2001.

Optimum Nutrition for the Mind, Patrick Holford, Piatkus, 2003.

Overcoming Depression, Paul Gilbert, Constable and Robinson, 2000.

Tai Chi, Paul Brecher, HarperCollins, 2000.

The New Raw Energy, Leslie and Susannah Kenton, Vermilion, 2001.

The Science of Homeopathy, George Vithoulkas, Grove Press, 1980

Yoga, Tantra and Meditation in Daily Life, Swami Janakananda Saraswati, Red Wheel/Weiser, 1992.

USEFUL ADDRESSES AND WEBSITES

UK
Alcoholics Anonymous (AA)
AA provides confidential and non-judgemental help to anyone with a drink problem. Their website gives details of meeting places.
tel: 0845 769 7555 (24 hour)
website: www.alcoholics-anonymous.org.uk
email: aanewcomer@runbox.com

Association for Post-natal Illness (APNI)
APNI provides support to mothers suffering from post-natal illness. For an information pack send an SAE to the address below.

145 Dawes Road
Fulham
London SW6 7EB
tel: 020 7386 0868
fax: 020 7386 8885
website: www.apni.org
email: info@apni.org

British Association for Behavioural and Cognitive Psychotherapies (BABCP)
Cognitive Behaviour Therapy is a practice which aims to help people experiencing a wide range of mental health difficulties. Send an SAE to the address below for a list of accredited practitioners.

Imperial House
Hornby Street
Bury
BL9 5BN
tel: 0161 705 4304
fax: 0161 705 4306
website: www.babcp.org.uk
email: babcp@babcp.com

British Association of Counselling and Psychotherapy (BACP)
A comprehensive reference point for anyone seeking information on

counselling and psychotherapy in the UK. Send an SAE for a list of accredited practitioners.

BACP House
15 St John's Business Park
Lutterworth
LE17 4HB
tel: 01455 883 300
fax: 01455 550 243
website: www.bacp.co.uk
email: bacp@bacp.co.uk

Cruse (Bereavement Care)
Cruse offers help to bereaved people through a free support service, opportunities for contact with others through bereavement support groups, and advice or information on practical matters.

tel: 0844 477 9400
website: www.crusebereavementcare.org.uk
email: info@cruse.org.uk

Electronic Healing Ltd
Suppliers of light boxes for those who suffer from SAD.

48 Surrenden Crescent
Brighton
East Sussex
BN1 6WF
tel: 0844 804 2130
fax: 0870 066 1921
website: www.electronichealing.co.uk

Fellowship of Depressives Anonymous (FDA)
FDA is a nationwide self-help organisation made up of individual members and groups which meet locally on a regular basis for mutual support.
Box FDA
c/o Self Help Nottingham
Ormiston House
32–36 Pelham Street
Nottingham NG1 2EG

tel: 0870 774 4320
fax: 0870 774 4319
website: www.depressionanon.co.uk
email: info@depressionuk.org

Mind (National Association for Mental Health)

Mind is the leading mental health charity in England and Wales. Its aim is to achieve a better life for everyone with experience of mental distress.

Mind
15–19 Broadway
London E15 4BQ
tel: 08457 660 163
fax: 020 8522 1725
website: www.mind.org.uk
email: contact@mind.org.uk

Narcotics Anonymous

NA is a support organisation for recovering drug addicts who meet regularly to help each other stay clean. Their website gives details of meetings.
tel: 0300 999 1212
website: www.ukna.org

Seasonal Affective Disorder Association (SADA)

SADA is a support organisation for those who suffer from Seasonal Affective Disorder.

SADA
PO Box 989
Steyning
West Sussex BN44 3HG
tel: 01903 814 942
fax: 01903 814 942
website: www.sada.org.uk

Australia

DepNet
DepNet is a depression information service for all Australians which aims to enable users to both understand the illness better and seek appropriate medical advice and treatment.
website: www.depnet.com.au
email: info@depnet.com.au

depressioNet
An online resource centre whose aim is to empower people to make informed choices and find solutions to the challenges of living with depression.

depressioNet
PO Box 57
Carlton South VIC 3053
tel: 03 9245 3030
website: www.depressioNet.com.au
email: team@depressioNet.com.au

Grow
An anonymous and confidential organisation which offers a 12-step self-help programme for those suffering with depression.

GROW National Centre
209A Edgeware Road
Enmore NSW 2042
tel: 02 9516 3733
fax: 02 9516 1503

Mental Health Information for Rural and Remote Australia
An information service for depression sufferers in rural and remote regions of Australia.
tel: 1300 785 005

New Zealand

The Mental Health Foundation of New Zealand
This website provides information and resources for sufferers of depression.
website: www.mentalhealth.org.nz

Singapore

Singapore Association for Counselling (SAC)
SAC provides information about the availability of treatment and psychotherapy in Singapore.

SAC
c/o Singapore Professional Centre
People's Association
West Block, Room W13, 9 Stadium Link
Singapore 397750
tel: 6348 2586/62
fax: 6440 9450
website: www.spc.org.sg

South Africa

Mental Health Information Centre of South Africa
This website provides information on depression and other mental illnesses, as well as treatment resources.
website: www.mentalhealth.co.za

Index